228

THEOLOGY AND
IN CONTEXT A

JOHN W. DE GRUCHY

Theology and Ministry in Context and Crisis

A South African Perspective

COLLINS

To
Desmond Mpilo Tutu
Pastor, Prophet and Theologian

Collins Liturgical Publications
8 Grafton Street, London W1X 3LA

Distributed in Ireland by
Educational Company of Ireland
21 Talbot Street, Dublin 1

Collins Liturgical Australia
PO Box 316, Blackburn, Victoria 3130

Distributed in Southern Africa by
Lux Verbi, Box 1822, Cape Town

ISBN 0 00 599969 3
© 1986 John de Gruchy
First published 1987

Grateful acknowledgement is made for permission to reproduce the
following copyright material: Mongane Serote for the poem 'Too much blood',
taken from *The Night Keeps Winking*.

Typeset by John Swain & Son
Printed by Wm Collins Sons & Co, Glasgow

Contents

Foreword

John de Gruchy operates in the 'context' and 'crisis' of
South Africa. Most of his readers do not. While his writing
appeals to thousands in South Africa, what he says here will
attract even more readers in the United Kingdom. There he
lectured on these subjects. He is also well known and well
read in the United States, whose 'contexts' he began to
know as a theological student years ago. Since then he has
frequently lectured in the United States.

Ministers in these and other nations know that they have
'contexts'. Whether they serve in industrial cities or on
farms, as hospital chaplains or parish pastors, through
denominations or ecumenical agencies, among rich or
poor, their setting helps determine how they minister.
Some of them have 'crises', as they, like many South African
counterparts, stare at the horrors of the time and try to do
something helpful in the face of them. For not a few ministers these may mean personal crises: of vocation, of faith, of
circumstance. Others take on issues that their societies
would rather see unaddressed, issues of justice and peace.
Most of them will not think of their contexts or crises as
being dramatic matches for those of South African ministers.

Does this mean that non-South Africans should read this
as a 'ministerial travel guide', a report on exotic and distant
places? Or — let me induce uneasiness in the mind of
author and publisher — does this mean that non-South
Africans will or should dismiss the book as being beside the
point for their ministry? I hope not, and all but guarantee

7

that anyone who gives the author a first few pages of opportunity will pursue his line of thought all the way.

What we are coming to learn, and what this book again makes clear, is that all ministry is contextual and set in particular crises. The Gospel is universal, the Church is ecumenical, and human needs can be general. Yet the Gospel always finds particular applications, the Church is always some place in some time, and human needs are as diverse as are humans and human groupings themselves. If we only wrote out of and to address our own contexts and crises, we would be solitaries or soliloquists, Robinson Crusoes of the faith at best and Narcissuses at worst. Instead, we have learned to hold up mirrors across cultures. We are learning to draw analogies across societies.

Think of this: the great books on theology and ministry are deeply rooted in particular contexts. We profit from Dietrich Bonhoeffer's works, on which de Gruchy has written as an expert, precisely because of their source in Finkenwalde, the underground seminary and the under-the-ban Confessing Church of Nazi Germany. In the United States people study Dorothy Day especially because of her location among the New York poor or on a Catholic Worker farm, or Martin Luther King as a black Baptist pastor in a southern city — even though these readers are far from such contexts. Reaching further back, it is important to see John Chrysostom (Chapter one, page one!) in his imperial setting, or Augustine as Bishop of Hippo. Who thinks of John Calvin without Geneva, of Luther without the Reformation struggle at Wittenburg?

When people forget context and crisis they turn abstract, detached, ideological, remote, unhelpful. When they remember context and crisis they show their identification with the people who are subjects and objects of Christian ministry. The situations they discuss become palpable, pulsing. When I read this manuscript I used one of those vivid yellow-green marking pens to heighten every appearance of the word 'South Africa'. The occurrences leap from the page. Then I reread the heightened paragraphs to see if anything in them was irrelevant in my contexts, because the people I know and I are one-third of a world away from South Africa. Not one line needed to be discarded and most lines were more vital, more vivid for the sense of immediacy they imparted. When we go deep enough into our circumstances, we find the strata where common human need and a common Gospel meet.

Professor de Gruchy knows that context and crisis produce souls under stress and resources for healing. He knows that context without a sense of crisis produces complacency, that crisis without context issues in alienation and dread loneliness. So he brings them together with 'theology', the interpretation of life and world and Word in which all Christians engage. And 'ministry', which is also all of theirs. Yet he has faith that theology born of and addressed to ordained ministerial needs has a special character. He lifts that up.

I cannot say that all his topics or treatments are utterly new. They became new because as a reader from far away I wanted to see what his context and crisis did to enliven ministry there, and then what was transportable. Again and again my unspoken response was, 'I'd never thought of it that way before!' Other readers are likely to have the same experience.

Readers who might feel they have no time to read this book because their contexts are complex, their crises demanding, would have second thoughts if they saw the circumstances in which it was written. It happened that I was in South Africa on the campus of the University of Cape Town next door to John de Gruchy's office as he put finishing touches on the work. At the time he was deaning, teaching, remaining involved with a local church and preaching to others, given to family concerns as its members shared the South African crisis. He was taking time to be a friend to my wife and me. There was always a conference that demanded a paper, a committee that deserved good attention, a cause that called forth people of courage and skill. Yet between all these things, this visitor, who found too many occasions to knock on his office door, also found that de Gruchy could turn right back to his word-processor and add a paragraph, delete another, polish still another. That kind of person one admires as someone who can teach us, and welcomes as one who knows how busy the rest of us are in theology and ministry. Those who cherish their hours will give a few to the reading of this book. I suggest some yellow-green underlinings and highlightings. They are going to want to consult it again and again, as contexts change, as crises go and come.

Martin E. Marty
The University of Chicago

Preface

For much of the past ten years I have been involved in
teaching theology, and increasingly in teaching ordained
ministers and priests, many of whom are doing graduate
studies while at the same time involved in parish and congregational work. Such students present a very special
challenge to the academic professor of theology. They
bring into the seminar room the daily struggles, frustra-
tions, and failures, but also the insights and victories of
their life and work. Many of them minister in extremely difficult situations, especially those who are black, situations
which have become particularly tense and even dangerous
in recent times. On several occasions I have been privileged
to teach students who have suffered greatly for their witness, some in prison and detention. In such situations theology has to be living and relevant to ministry; there is
neither the time nor the space, or even the inclination for
theological abstraction or dilettantism. Moreover, theology under such circumstances cannot be trendy, superficial
or peripheral to the central themes of the gospel and the
Christian tradition, or unrelated to the historical context
and its crises, for then it will fail to provide the resources
necessary for ministry. This conviction, perhaps more than
any other, lies at the centre of what I have attempted to write
about in this book.

The substance of what follows has been fermenting for a
fairly long time in my own thinking and experience as a
pastor and teacher. However, the immediate cause for
attempting to express my thoughts on the subject was an

invitation by the Principal and Senatus of Westminster College, Cambridge, to present the James Reid Memorial Lectures in June 1986. The regulations for these Lectures specifically state that they 'shall be related to or deal with some aspect of the life and work of the ordained ministry of the church.' Thus the focus of the book is upon the ordained ministry, whatever its designation within the different Christian traditions. It should be clear at the outset, however, that I regard the ministry of the church as the prerogative and responsibility of all its members. I would certainly not wish to reinforce in any way the clericalism that still prevails in many sections of the church. In order to make this clear, I have used the phrase 'ordained ministry' throughout the text when referring to the ministry of the Word and Sacraments or, in the Catholic tradition, the priesthood. Ministry as such refers to the task of the whole People of God, and it is by no means confined to the institutional church. In discussing the ordained ministry, I have not distinguished between various orders (e.g. bishop, priest, deacon). These can be made and applied where appropriate according to the specific tradition of the reader.

The invitation from Westminster College also asked that I should keep in mind the context, namely Britain, in which the majority of those who would hear the lectures exercise their ministry. And yet, at the same time, I was requested to reflect on the issues out of my own experience as a theologian and minister in South Africa today. The latter request tied in directly with my own conviction that something needed to be written on practical theology in South Africa which would be of value to those struggling to be faithful pastors and priests in our present critical context. This was reflected in the recommendations of the Report of the Human Sciences Research Council, *Religion, Intergroup Relations and Social Change in South Africa* in 1985 which stated:

There is a need to develop a more adequate pastoral theology and practice in order to provide pastoral care in a
rapidly changing society, characterised by uncertainty,
insecurity and social crisis. Care should be taken that an
effective ministry is provided for needs both on the personal and sociopolitical level.[1]

Partly in response to this recommendation I had already
applied for a research grant from the Human Sciences
Research Council to enable me to undertake such a task.
Work on the Reid Lectures became part of that undertak-
ing, but the project also includes the preparation of a more
detailed research report and, it is anticipated, a resource
volume on practical theology in South Africa.

Undoubtedly the word 'crisis', used in the title, has been
overworked. There is no other word, however, which is
adequate to express the moment of judgment that is upon
South Africa at present. The crisis, of course, is also one
which directly affects the church and the ordained ministry
in South Africa, indeed, the first letter of Peter in the New
Testament suggests that judgment begins with the 'house-
hold of faith'. Biblically-speaking, a crisis is not only a
moment of judgment in history but also a moment of opportunity and decision which can lead to repentance, transformation and renewal. It is my hope that this book may
contribute to this ever necessary process of renewal
within the church and its ministry.

The word 'contextual' suffers from the same overexpo-
sure as does 'crisis', and yet it conveys most adequately
what it signifies. The crisis in the church and ministry in the
South African context is directly related to a country in crisis. A theology of ministry has therefore to be worked out
in relation to our particular historical situation and its
demands. As such it needs to be a theology of ministry
which relates not only to black and white pastors and con-

gregations, not only to urban and rural situations, but also to the urgent demand for social justice and transformation which arises as much from the gospel of the kingdom of God as it does from the cries of the poor and the oppressed.

The fact that research and reflection needs to be contextual does not mean, of course, that the insights which may emerge are of no wider interest. On the contrary, it can be argued that it is precisely reflections that are rooted in particular historical and concrete situations that have universal significance. William Burrows, a Roman Catholic missiologist and theologian aptly writes:

> Aside from concrete social, material, and historical contexts, there exist only abstract principles. One of the problems in thinking about the church has been the tendency to consider it universally and abstractly, without coming to grips with the contextual factors that alone give flesh to its mission in concrete historical and cultural situations. To decontextualize anything is to rob it of what makes it either interesting or important, and any attempt to deal with the church from universalist perspectives makes it difficult to come to grips with important contextual factors which *intrinsically* affect the church's mission.[2]

What I have attempted, however, is not only to inject some insights arising from our situation and my own experience into the general debate about the ministry of the church and the ordained ministry in particular, but also to relate that debate to the issues facing us in South Africa. Thus the material with which I have worked has been drawn from a wide variety of sources both local and universal, Catholic and Protestant, traditional and contemporary. South Africa provides a unique context for doing theology, not only because of the issues, but also because of the interaction of so many diverse expressions of Christian faith and practice in our midst. My own perspective has clearly been shaped

14

by a more Reformed understanding of theology and ministry, for which I make no apology. This means that my orientation is what some would call a 'Word of God' theology,
that is, a theology in which the witness of Scripture is normative. But I have also been privileged to drink from the
wells of other traditions. Behind them all, I believe, lies a
common commitment to being faithful to the witness of the
Biblical tradition.

What follows is not a comprehensive theology of ministry nor a detailed programme for theological education, but
a contribution from within the South African context to the
world-wide debate on the ordained ministry.

My main focus is upon the ordained minister as practical
theologian. As pastor, prophet, preacher or liturgist, the
ordained minister provides the theological direction for the
People of God engaged in mission in the world.

Included in the book are the three James Reid Memorial
Lectures, now substantially revised, and a revised version
of the C.B. Powell Lecture which I gave at the University of
South Africa in October 1985. This was originally entitled
'Standing by God in his Hour of Grieving: Human Suffering, Theological Reflection and Christian Solidarity.' The
discussion in this essay is integral to issues raised in the
other chapters, and it illustrates the way in which I believe
theological reflection can relate to Christian ministry and
witness. Also embodied in the substance of the book are
many insights which I have gained from students and colleagues during the past months as we have worked together
in research and teaching. I am also mindful of what I have
been taught by the several congregations where I have
served as pastor since my ordination in 1961.

Thanks are due in particular to Principal Martin Cressey
and the Senatus of Westminster College, Cambridge, for
the gracious invitation to present the James Reid Memorial

Lectures, and also to Martin and Pam Cressey for their warm and generous hospitality during the two weeks my wife and I spent in their home. I am also grateful to other members of the Cambridge Theological Federation, both students and faculty who participated in the lectures, and who, by their searching and helpful questions and comments have undoubtedly contributed to making this a better book. Thanks are also due to the C.B. Powell Bible Centre and its Director, Professor Pieter de Villiers, for permission to include a revised version of my Powell Lecture; to Nan Oosthuizen without whose secretarial skills I would be greatly handicapped; to Denise Ackermann, James Cochrane and Robin Petersen, for their insights and comments; and to the Human Sciences Research Council for their generous grant for the practical theology research project. Martin Marty, the Fairfax M. Cone Distinguished Service Professor of the History of Modern Christianity at the University of Chicago, not only kindly agreed to write the Foreword, but also made many helpful comments while reading the penultimate version of the manuscript during his visit to the University of Cape Town in August 1986. Sue and Geoffrey Chapman and their staff at Collins, London, have as always been most helpful, and I am indebted to them not only for their professional skills but also for their personal support and enthusiasm.

John W. de Gruchy
Cape Town,
September 1986

CHAPTER ONE

Ministry, Theology, and the Community of Faith

Changing Images of Ministry

Tucked away in his introduction to St John Chrysostom's fourth century *Treatise on the Priesthood* is this comment, written a hundred years ago, by the North American church historian Philip Schaff:

> This book is the most useful or at least the best known among the works of Chrysostom, and it is well calculated to inspire a profound sense of the tremendous responsibilities of the ministry. But it has serious defects ... and cannot satisfy the demands of an evangelical minister. In all that pertains to the proper care of souls it is inferior to the *Reformed Pastor* of Richard Baxter.[1]

Depending upon one's own perspective, Schaff may or may not be correct in his opinions, but he certainly had a clear understanding of what he believed the ordained ministry should be, as did John Chrysostom and Richard Baxter, the seventeenth century Puritan divine.

Thirteen centuries separate the world of Chrysostom and that of Baxter, centuries which include the Great Schism between Rome and Chrysostom's own see of Constantinople, the Protestant Reformation, several fundamental shifts in Christian and secular thought, and a myriad of significant events in social history. Their contexts and cultures were very different, more different perhaps than Philip Schaff recognised in assessing their respective merits. Chrysostom's vision of ministry was Byzantine, priestly and ascetic; Baxter's was English, reformed and middle-

class. When you examine the texts, however, there are continuities between the two, as, indeed there are between
them and more traditional understandings of ministry
today. For one thing, both think of the ordained ministry in
terms of what Edward Farley has called 'the clerical paradigm'.[2] Baxter's 'new presbyter' is no less clerical, than
Chrysostom's 'old priest'. Furthermore, it would have been
far beyond the bounds of their contemplation that the
ordained ministry could be anything but male.

Despite the vast historical, cultural and theological gulf
which separates us today from Chrysostom and Baxter
their respective images of the ordained ministry – the
priestly and the Reformed pastor – continue to shape the
way in which this ministry is understood. Consider, for
example, the Vatican II 'Decree on the Ministry and Life
of Priests', and John Paul II's very moving 'Letter to
Priests' on the occasion of his enthronement as bishop
of Rome in which he wrote:

> This is the 'supreme art' to which Jesus Christ has called
> you. 'The supreme art is the direction of souls', wrote Saint
> Gregory the Great. I say to you, therefore, using this
> phraseology: endeavour to be 'artists' of pastoral work.[3]

Though Baxter's heirs, and the heirs of the Reformation
generally, would object to the title priest, few would object
to this vision of ministry. Indeed, Dietrich Bonhoeffer, the
German Lutheran theologian, pastor, and martyr at the
hands of the Gestapo, was deeply attracted by the image of
the Catholic priest portrayed in the novels of Georges
Bernanos, the author of *The Diary of a Country Priest*.[4] Nevertheless, for him, the focus for the 'cure of souls' was not the
sacraments, but the proclamation of the Word of God.[5] The
primary image of the ordained minister as Reformed and
Lutheran pastor is not the priest hearing confessions and

celebrating the eucharist but the ministry of the Word and Sacraments in which the proclamation of the Word of God takes precedence.

Although these two powerful images of the ordained ministry, the priest and the minister of the Word, continue to shape the self-understanding of ordained ministers today, there is ample evidence that many priests and pastors are not at all sure of their vocational identity. Sometimes, they take the images for granted, even hiding behind them, without really thinking them through and seeking to embody them in their particular historical context. What, for example, does it really mean to be a priest or a Reformed preacher of the Word of God in South Africa today? Some even reject such images as outmoded, and seek to replace them with ones which seem more appropriate to the contemporary world and its demands.

Almost ten years ago Stewart Ranson, Alan Bryman and Bob Hinings published their study on the identity and role of clergy in England entitled *Clergy, Ministers & Priests*. In the epilogue to their report these three social scientists concluded:

> So the ordained ministry is decidedly an occupation in flux. The parish priest, the incumbent, or circuit minister, occupies a frontline position in an organisation whose secular relevance is questioned from without and whose traditions are threatened from within. This prominence at the same time makes him particularly vulnerable, for he is the person who most acutely experiences the frustrations of the Churches' questionable relevance in the modern world.

On the basis of their survey, Ranson, Bryman and Hinings continued:

> In response to these disenchanting experiences, he can choose *inter alia* to redefine the nature of his ministry. He can seek to make it 'relevant', either by leaving the ministry

19

and moving into one of the 'helping and caring' professions, or by redefining the nature of his ministry *qua* clergyman or whatever.[6]

While a great deal has been said and written about the ordained ministry during the past decade, especially by Roman Catholic theologians, there still remains uncertainty about the precise identity, role and relevance of the ordained ministry, an uncertainty often related to particular socio-political crises. Consider the conclusion which Sydney Ahlstrom reaches in the final chapter of the revised edition of the study by H. Richard Niebuhr and Daniel Day Williams on *The Ministry in Historical Perspective*. Written within the North American context, the chapter is appropriately entitled 'The Ministry from the Placid Decade to the Present: 1950-1980'. Ahlstrom concludes that it is not surprising that recent research has discovered 'a prevailing uncertainty among ministers, both as to their purpose and their capability in a rapidly changing world'.[7] Joseph Hough and John Cobb put it more sharply in their recent study on *Christian Identity and Theological Education:*

> Confusion about the ministry has increased. Reeling under the impact of post-Neo-orthodox theological criticism and the resulting cacophony of theological voices, and working in congregations with vastly differing expectations, it is little wonder that ministers find no authoritative basis for their profession.[8]

The uncertainty takes different forms within Catholic and Protestant churches because of traditional differences in their respective conceptions of the ordained ministry. But even so, there is a commonality in the uncertainty which embraces most denominations. The questions which Hans Kung dealt with in his little book *Why Priests?* in 1971 are questions which many Protestant ministers ask as well.[9]

One reason suggested for this is precisely that which we have already intimated – the various images which have guided ministers in the past in shaping their self-under-standing and work have disintegrated, with 'the consequent fragmentation of ministerial practice'.[10]

The fact is that in spite of important continuities in the self-understanding of the ordained ministry, it cannot escape the forces of history and cultural change. Indeed, the understanding and practice of ministry in the Christian church has changed considerably during the past two thousand years. Even within Catholic circles what is meant by the word 'priest' has undergone significant transforma-tion.[11] If we include the changes which have occurred outside the Roman Catholic tradition, it is possible to discern a greater number, even though they may all be contained within the general designation of 'preacher of the Word.' In his *Theology of Ministry*, the Dominican Thomas O'Meara describes what he calls 'six metamor-phoses which ministry has undergone' during the past two millenia. He writes:

> Two thousand years lie between the pneumatic, mis-sionary churches of the first century and the ministries we need at this moment as history nears the end of the second millennium. This span between the first and twentieth cen-turies is not a void, nor a linear distribution of museums. History is a living drama where old and new characters act out their play, the one drama of grace. The different epochs of history have touched and transformed Christian minis-try. The Gospel in theology and the church in ministry have not hesitated to become incarnate in various cultures.[12]

From a North American Protestant perspective Ronald Osborn has shown how, in the course of American history, dominant ministerial types have emerged which have defined the profession for their time. He refers especially to the 'Master' (the Scottish 'dominee'), the 'Revivalist', the 'Pulpiteer' ('princes of the pulpit'), and the 'Builder' (the organizer and motivater). These 'ministerial characters'

> arose in relation to certain theological concepts of the church and ministry resident in the Christian tradition, as those concepts were influenced by the churches' peculiar socio-historical locations. A particular character arose and became embedded in the minds of church people and widely recognised both within and outside of the church. The character then receded in importance, as both theological and socio-cultural movements interacted to give birth to a new 'character'.[13]

Within the South African context it is likewise possible to distinguish an array of similar 'ministerial characters' which provide a model for theological students, ordained ministers, and theological educators, and relate to the expectations of both congregations and the world at large. Though often caricatured, these would include the Afrikaner 'dominee', the 'political priest', the pentecostal revivalist preacher, and the African indigenous church bishop or prophet. Each of these has arisen within a specific cultural and historical context, and is as much influenced by that as it is by theology and Christian tradition.

In his classic study on *The Christian Ministry in Africa*, written in 1960 at the beginning of the end of colonialism in Africa, Bengt Sundkler commented that the ministry in the African church was not so much determined by a contextual theology appropriate to the situation, but by inherited missionary models.

> It is not so much the professed and verbally expressed theology of the ministry that is shaping the attitude of African office-bearers. It is rather the phenomenology of the ministry: that which was *seen* and observed in the actual

practice of the missionary and his first African co-workers conditions their outlook. If the Westerner largely represented the minister to be an efficient administrator, *or* an ordained school inspector, *or* an excellent and painstaking accountant, *or* an interested master-builder and architect, *or* again, an impressive combination of mechanic and preacher, these patterns will influence his younger African colleagues and to some extent determine their conception of the ministry.

Sundkler went on to say, however, that something new was beginning to emerge, something of an African pattern of ministry shaped by the needs of the church within the African context and its particular sociological conditions.[14]

What Sundkler perceived emerging was an understanding of ministry in which the images of priest (if the tradition was Catholic) or pastor (if Protestant) were meshed with traditional African ideas of representative and charismatic leadership, ideas which are clearly evident also within the Bible. As representative leader, the ordained minister stands between the flock and the tribe; as charismatic leader, he or she stands in the tradition of the Apostles, speaking, leading and healing with their authority. It is difficult to discern the extent to which this pattern of ordained ministry has in fact been realised. The diversity of the church in South Africa alone, with its often very different images of the ordained ministry, is sufficient to prevent us from making generalisations. Nevertheless, Sundkler's observation appears to be true in many instances, not only but not least within the African indigenous churches.

Protestants in particular have taken the ordained ministry too much for granted, assuming perhaps that we have a clear grasp of its identity and task. There was, indeed, much critical reflection, especially in the sixties, but a great deal of it resulted in a secularised self-understanding within the ranks of the ordained ministry: an understanding totally unrelated to the church in Africa, though it appealed to some white priests and ministers in South Africa as it did in Europe and North America. This had several consequences. It led some to leave the ordained ministry; it contributed to the emergence of the charismatic renewal within the churches, as ministers sought to regain a spiritual foundation for their vocation; and it produced amongst some a conservative, uncritical reaction. Whatever its consequences, however, it has also forced us to recognise the identity crisis facing the ordained ministry, and to rework the traditional understanding of ministry in relation to the renewal and mission of the church within our contemporary situations.

At a time of crisis for the church in South Africa and other parts of the world, a time when we are also reaching for ecumenical consensus on the ordained ministry, as for example in the Faith and Order document of the World Council of Churches, *Baptism, Eucharist and Ministry*, but also at a time when we are concerned about the renewal of the church and its mission, we dare not overlook the restatement of what we mean by the ministry of the Word and Sacraments. It is not simply questions of church order and ordination that should concern us in a theology of ministry, but the *vocation* of the ordained ministry, its theological identity and task in the modern world, especially in situations of social crisis. Unfortunately, because the problem of order has dominated ecumenical discussion on the ordained ministry, working towards consensus on a common understanding of the vocation of the ordained ministry in these terms has had much less emphasis. Yet the ecumenical movement has brought into a new relationship a wealth of experience and understanding in regard to the ordained ministry as a vocation, especially from the third world, which should enrich any attempt to develop a theology and practice of ministry.

The pastoral and prophetic responsibilities of the ordained ministry, the 'cure of souls' and the proclamation of the Word of God, derive from the calling to enable people to know, trust and obey God in Jesus Christ. This requires relating Christian faith to contemporary situations, a communicative task best described as practical theology. The model of the ordained minister as *practical theologian* transcends the historic division in which the priest is primarily the celebrant of the mass and the Reformed pastor the preacher of the Word, though, of course, the priest also preaches the Word and the Reformed pastor also celebrates the sacraments. These distinct emphases remain, but priest and pastor find their commonality in providing direction to the community of faith engaged in mission in the world. It is a model, I suggest, which also relates to that which Sundkler saw emerging in Africa, a model in which the ordained minister was both a representative and charismatic leader of the People of God.

Ministry within the Community of Faith

There are traditions within the Christian church which reject the need for an ordained ministry. This protest by communities stemming from the Radical Reformation, such as the Quakers, is a salutary warning against a narrow and false understanding of the Christian ministry. For our purposes, however, I am affirming, with justification I believe, that what has been traditionally called the ministry of the Word and Sacraments is both biblically and theologically based, and is necessary for the life and witness of the church. This does not mean, of course, that all understandings of the ordained ministry or the historical forms which it has taken are equally acceptable.

Although my focus is upon the calling and task of the ordained ministry, I must state very clearly, then, that this should not be understood as support for any form of clericalism. On the contrary, clericalism is one of the moulds into which social pressure has, in the course of history, pushed the ordained ministry, and from which it needs to be rescued. It is tragic that clericalism remains rife today despite the emphasis that has been placed upon the ministry of the laity within mainline Christianity during this century. Bengt Sundkler even discerned 'an unmistakeable tendency towards clericalism' within the church in Africa which, he rightly argued, would undermine the vision of ministry as representative and charismatic leadership.[15]

But clericalism is not overcome by rejecting an ordained ministry or by down-playing its significance and task. The church requires strong leadership, both pastoral and theological, at all times, but especially in times of crisis. Edward Schillebeeckx, critical of clericalism as he is, points out that 'if there is no specialized concentration of what is important to everyone, in the long run the community suffers as a result.'[16] All Christians, for example, are meant to be practical theologians, evangelists or priests, but some have a special calling, particular gifts, and are especially trained to fulfil such tasks within the body of Christ. In reflecting on the rediscovery of the ministry of the laity within the ecumenical movement, Hans-Ruedi Weber once pertinently remarked: 'A high doctrine of the laity includes rather than excludes a high doctrine of the ordained ministry.' He went on to say:

> The important thing is that the nature and task of the laity
> is no more defined by comparing them with a special group

within the Church – the ordained clergy, the theologian, the professional church worker – but by a new appreciation of the Church in the world.[17]

In the New Testament and early Christian tradition the ordained ministry is always understood as something which exists only within the community of faith. It is never conceived of as existing prior to or independent of the church, nor as something above the local church, but as one form of ministry amongst others existing both for the building up of the church and its mission in the world. In fact, the identity of the ordained ministry is bound up with the identity of the church, and its task with the task of the church. Thus in order to understand what is meant by the ministry of the Word and Sacraments we have to ask first about its location within the total ministry of the church, and, second, about the mission of the church in the world.

The ordained ministry, or, ministry of the Word and Sacraments, is only one form of ministry within the community of faith. Schillebeeckx, in reflecting on the ministry in the early Christian communities reminds us that this diversity of ministry was, however, soon lost in the process of institutionalisation. He writes:

> The development of ministry in the early Christian churches was not so much, as is sometimes claimed, a historical shift from charisma to institution but a shift from the charisma of many to a specialized charisma of just a few.[18]

Thus, for example, the diaconate, instead of being a ministry in its own right, became a stepping-stone to the priesthood and remained such within the Catholic tradition until Vatican II.

In seeking the reformation of the church in the sixteenth century, some of the Protestant Reformers, especially Calvin, recognised the need for such diversity and restructured the church accordingly. Lay people, for example, were brought into the centre of the ministry of the church in the office of elder and deacon. Distinctions were also made in some Reformed churches between teaching elders and ruling elders, so that the work of preaching and teaching was separated from that of governing the church. In the Second Helvetic Confession (1566), which has been formative for the Reformed tradition, we are told that the ordained ministry 'is not to be despised' (chapter 18). But in the very next paragraph we are warned not to 'attribute too much to ministers and the ministry'. Yet the diversity of ministry often became more a matter of form and order rather than a dynamic ministry in its own right, and the caution of the Second Helvetic Confession was not always borne in mind. Protestant pastors became *the* ministry in the church, princes of the pulpit, managers of the congregation and executives of the denomination, even if not Cardinals within a medieval Curia.

The Pauline tradition of a 'tent-making' ministry indicates that the distinct tasks of the ordained ministry do not necessarily require a full-time appointment, and that there are advantages in what some call supplementary ministries. The ministry of the Word and Sacraments does not imply *functioning* full-time, though it does require *being* full-time as is required of any Christian disciple. In many situations, however, the minister of the Word and Sacraments has had to fulfil a variety of roles tangential to his or her calling because the ordained minister has often been the best educated person in the community. In some contexts this may still be true and is not to be disparaged. But in many situations where it is no longer necessary, some find it difficult to surrender roles which are not essential to their vocation. Or else they try to carve out new niches in society which will give them a feeling of relevance and, in the process, demonstrate their importance to the wider community. This not only denies the ministry of the whole people of God within the world, but it also and inevitably detracts from and undermines the specific vocation of the ordained minister.

A 'team ministry' of ordained ministers is often necessary and helpful within a city or social region. Indeed, my understanding of the ordained minister as practical theologian implies that he or she is part of a wider group of theologians, and not an isolated unit working alone. However, the primary 'team ministry' is not the working together of ordained professionals, but the complementary exercising of all the gifts of ministry within the community of faith. Only within this context, as Hans Kung indicates, can we begin to ask the question 'why priests' or ordained ministers?[19] The ministry of the Word and Sacraments finds its meaningful, rightful and yet distinct place within this complex of ministries. Moreover, the fourth article of the Barmen Declaration of the Confessing Church in Germany rightly reminds us:

> The various offices in the Church do not establish a dominion of some over others; on the contrary, they are for the exercise of the ministry entrusted to and enjoined upon the whole congregation.

The ministry of the church is that of Jesus Christ through the Spirit. This ministry is given to the whole church and to a variety of people within it. The need to recapture this New Testament vision and practice of ministry has been strongly emphasised in our century by the independent churches in Africa, the Charismatic renewal movement within the mainline churches, the base communities within Latin America, some Vatican II decrees, World Council of

Churches studies on ministry and the laity, and is affirmed by theologians of many different traditions in their studies on ministry. Any other view is contrary to the New Testament and the best in Christian tradition; it results in a truncated, inadequate and impoverished ministry. The ministry of the church as a whole builds up the church in faith and love, and helps to equip it for mission in the world.

Just as the ordained ministry does not exist independently of the church, or separate from the ministry of the body of Christ as a whole, so the church does not exist for its own sake. It exists in order to bear witness in the world to the transforming gospel of the kingdom of God in the life, ministry, death and resurrection of Jesus Christ through the enabling power of the Holy Spirit. This defines the relationship of the church to the world, and provides the basis and orientation for its task in the world. It also helps us delineate more clearly the identity and task of the ordained ministry. While there are contentious and complex theological issues at stake here, we must necessarily take a few short-cuts and make some affirmations.

The mission of the church, in bearing witness to the gospel of the kingdom of God, concerns God's transformation of societies and people so that they may mirror more clearly God's purposes of justice and love, liberation and reconciliation, righteousness, wholeness and peace. The participation of the church in this *missio Dei* is thus primarily that of evangelism, but evangelism understood in terms of the total message of God's kingdom. The false dualisms of Platonism and the Enlightenment, which result in a pseudo-piety in which faith and politics, body and soul are wrenched apart, are to be rejected at the outset as unbiblical and destructive of the mission of the church in bearing witness to the kingdom of God. This mission is at once, therefore, an integrated or holistic task related, for example, both

30

to the liberation of the oppressed and poor, and to the birth of a living and renewing faith in Jesus Christ. In word and deed the church is called to bear witness to Jesus Christ as Lord, saviour and liberator.

What then is the distinct role of the ordained ministry? The ordained ministry exists to equip the community of faith for its world-centred task, and its particular contribution in this regard should be that of providing the church with direction for that task. *Baptism, Eucharist and Ministry* speaks of 'the chief responsibility of the ordained ministry' as assembling and building 'up the body of Christ by proclaiming and teaching the Word of God, by celebrating the sacraments, and by guiding the life of the community in its worship, its mission and its caring ministry'.[20] Although I am aware of the debate surrounding this paragraph within the Commission on Faith and Order, I would still prefer to change the order here. The chief task of the ordained ministry is guiding the life of the community in worship, mission and caring through preaching and teaching the Word of God and celebrating the sacraments. 'Being a minister' Leonardo Boff reminds us, 'basically has to do with the direction of the community'.[21] This is the task of theological discernment and leadership, central tasks of the practical theologian.

The Ministry in Context

The ordained ministry, as an integral part of the church in the world, must be related to the socio-political and cultural context within which it exists. Hence its character and style may well change not only from one generation to the next but also from one social location to the next even within the same country. The fact that these changes sometimes take place imperceptibly rather than by careful planning or design does not deny their reality. The process of adaptation derives from the very nature of the gospel itself which seeks to transform people and societies within their historical context.

During the social crisis in South Africa in 1985, the problems which emanated from apartheid and confronted many pastors in their congregations, whether white or black, intensified and took on new dimensions. Many pastors in the black community were drawn, often reluctantly but sometimes in the vanguard, into the thick of the action in the townships. On top of the normal daily trials of living within the apartheid system, they now had to relate to a struggle led by students and the trade unions, often in tension with the more conservative membership of their churches. Somehow they had to minister to young radicals and their more cautious parents, and they had to do so in the context of increasing violence as protest led to confrontation with the authorities and sparked off the familiar spiral of violence. The task of burying the dead in many instances was transformed from the usual pastoral situation into a religious and political event. At many different levels they were caught in the cross-fire of a tense and deteriorating situation, in which, moreover, the Christian faith and the church itself was being radically questioned. Christian commitment to non-violent strategies and a gospel of reconciliation were under attack, forcing pastors to grapple with issues for which they had often not been trained. The whole context of their ministry was being dramatically transformed by the crisis, and they were being challenged to do theology in a way which was often very different to that taught in the seminaries.

At the same time, white pastors in the more affluent suburban and city congregations had the opposite problem to face, at least if they were attempting to be faithful to the gospel. Here the problem was that of trying to be a prophet and a pastor at the same time. Challenging white privilege and self-interest for the sake of the gospel, calling for repentance and fundamental change in support of the struggle for justice, and yet maintaining the unity of the fellowship and ministering to the fears, uncertainties and strains of life which had intensified as a result of the crisis. The gap between prophetic synodical resolutions and the interests of members of the congregation severely taxed the resources of the ministry if pastors defended and applied the stand taken by their churches. Many of those who agreed with the resolutions, and there were those who did not, avoided the issues in order to keep the peace. But the socio-political situation impinged even on the normal round of pastoral duties, even if pastors were not aware of the inter-relatedness of personal and social crises. The ordinary task of caring for families in danger of divorce, for example, took on a new dimension as couples had to struggle with their own problems in the context of general uncertainty and growing stress. The counselling of young people called up into the military to serve in the black townships, or young people deciding to leave the country for elsewhere, or young people detained by the police, made youth and student ministry far more demanding and immediate than it is in more relaxed times. Like their black colleagues in ministry, white pastors were hardly trained to cope with such situations, either theologically or pastorally. Moreover, neither they nor their congregations could be neutral, they had to take sides, even if they were not aware that they were doing so. This was not only a frustrating situation because of the feeling of impotence, but when taken seriously it could be very costly. Whether serving in black or white contexts, pastors seeking to be faithful to the gospel could not stand aside or opt out of the situation.

Thus the character which the ordained ministry takes within South Africa can vary greatly depending upon the immediate context within which one has to minister, and the same is true in other countries and situations. Ministry in a black township, the inner city, or a more affluent white suburb will take on different forms or emphases. This is evangelically necessary; it is the apostolic calling to be 'all things to all people'. But this does not mean that there should be no congruence between them: contextuality does not exclude but requires and makes universality meaningful. The ministries of both black and white pastors in South Africa should relate integrally to each other in terms of the mission of the church even though they may minister in different ways. And it is equally important that the ministry of the church in, say Europe or North America, is not unrelated to that in South Africa. This is what Joseph Hough and John Cobb mean by the 'global context' of ministry. 'To minister at any place in the world without regard for how that ministry is related to God's comprehensive activity is insufficient and can work against rather than with God.'[22] To minister in any one place requires an awareness of the universal mission of the church; and yet, at the same time, that task has to be grounded in each specific situation. The universality of the ordained ministry as the ministry of Jesus Christ demands that there be a common commitment, a common vision and a common sharing in the witness to the kingdom of God. The contextuality of the ordained ministry requires that this commonality become concrete in particular places in relation to the needs and struggles of the People of God.

Formally, throughout much of historic Christendom, the call of Christ to the ordained ministry has to be ratified both by an ecclesiastical hierarchy or synod representing the universal church of Jesus Christ, and by the call of the people of God in a particular place. This affirms the need for order and authority in the church as well as acceptance by a particular community of faith. But it also affirms the universality and the contextuality of this ministry which derives from both the nature of the gospel and the nature of the church. The ecclesial context of the ordained ministry is at the same time the church universal and a local community of faith. The ordained ministry is the gift of Jesus Christ to the church as a whole, but a gift that has to be exercised in a particular time and place.

One of the most remarkable features of Leonardo Boff's recent *Ecclesiogenesis*,[23] subtitled 'The base communities reinvent the church', is that despite its undeniably Catholic presuppositions, its focus is often congregationalist. No wonder the Vatican became anxious about Boff's theology! But Boff's stress on the local community of faith is in continuity with the teaching of the Vatican II *Decree on the Dogmatic Constitution of the Church* (article 26), and he is not alone among Catholic theologians in placing the emphasis at this point. Indeed, Nicholas Lash is of the opinion 'that none of the changes in Catholic Christianity which have occurred in recent decades are of more far-reaching potential significance than what we might call the recovery of the "congregationalist" element in Catholicism'.[24]

This rediscovery of the local community of faith by Catholic theologians comes at a time when many of us who are Congregationalists by tradition have learnt to stress more strongly the catholicity of the church. The local community of faith cannot exist except as part of the universal church. And yet, the whole church is present in the local community. Congregationalist theologian P.T. Forsyth expressed this in his *The Church and the Sacraments* at the beginning of the century. Forsyth was concerned to develop an organic understanding of the church as both catholic and congregational, an ecclesiology in which the dangers of both traditions are overcome. In firmly rejecting independency and the rampant individualism that goes with much of it, he insisted: 'The Church in a private house was as much *the* Church as the whole Christianity of Corinth.' Forsyth did so because he was opposed to the reduction of the local church to the level of a branch office of some denomination that had no sense of being the church and fulfilling its mission in its particular locality. He was affirming the corporate, organic nature of the church universal and local.[25] Compare this with Lash's comment:

> It has begun to dawn on us that when a group of people express, in the breaking of bread, hope sprung from the memory of the Crucified, then – however small and undistinguished the company, however ritually unimpressive the circumstances – *what* they are is not a 'bit' of something bigger, not an obscure branch office of a multinational corporation, but, quite simply, the church of Christ, in its entirety.[26]

Despite the similarities, there are some important differences between Boff's ecclesiology and Lash's portrait of a 'base community', and traditional Congregationalism. Not the least of these is that while Boff's local communities of faith are comprised of the poor, Congregationalists like others within much of mainline European or North American Christianity have generally been comfortable and middle-class. While this is not always true any longer as, for example, within South Africa itself where most Congregationalists are black, it raises in an urgent way the question of the identity of the local church or community of faith as the context for ministry.

36

The contemporary emphasis in liberation theology on 'the church of the poor' and 'base communities' is not only a necessary corrective to traditional ecclesiology and praxis, but also an affirmation of something central to the ecclesiology of the New Testament and therefore to its understanding of ministry.[27] When we speak of the local church we must not, therefore, immediately jump to the conclusion that this refers solely to the kind of suburban congregation or parish church with which most of us are familiar. Such remain important expressions of the local church, but they are not exclusively so. Often such local churches deny the catholicity of the church simply because they are so clearly bound to particular racial and cultural groups as well as economic classes. Concomitantly, the ordained ministry becomes equally bound to the same social forces instead of representing the universal church of Jesus Christ in that place.

This is a particular problem for the church in South Africa where apartheid has radically divided people and kept them apart on the basis of race, class and culture. The Group Areas Act, for example, has ensured community segregation to such an extent that it is usually practically impossible for any local church to be non-racial, even though this may be possible in theory and, in exceptional situations, in practice. Ordained ministers often end up serving particular groups, indeed, becoming captive to them and their interests rather than being ministers of the church of Jesus Christ. But South Africa is only an extreme example of what is a universal phenomenon: cultural, class and ethnic uniformity and interests have been determinative for the shaping of many congregations in most parts of the world.

Thus, while it is evangelically necessary for the ordained ministry to relate to its particular historical and cultural

37

context, we also need to be aware that cultural adaptation often occurs in ways which are detrimental to ministry and mission. This derives from the fact that every ordained minister belongs to a particular nation, ethnic group, class, and local social and ecclesial community. Herein lies the danger of acculturation. In the same way as the church has so often succumbed to the pressures of society and conformed to its norms, the world has squeezed the ordained ministry into its mould. 'Ministerial characters' too often reflect models of secular leadership, and conform to expectations that are unworthy of the gospel and contrary to the ministry of Jesus Christ.

Due, in part, to the insights of the sociology of knowledge, we are more aware today of the effect which our position within society has on our attitudes, perceptions and actions, and how it shapes our theology. In South Africa black and white perceptions are often radically different, not only within society or the church at large, but also within the ranks of the ordained ministry and church leadership more generally. Any theology of ministry or any programme of theological education which fails to take this into critical account must end up in some form of cultural captivity. For this very reason the social location of the ordained ministry becomes an important fact in assessing its character and task, and in understanding its reaction and response to contemporary issues and crises. Without necessarily realising it, ordained ministers are often in bondage to their own ethnic and class interests and values. Thus critical self-knowledge is essential in thinking about and practising our calling within our respective historical situations and their crises. For the sake of the church and its task, the ordained ministry must be contextual yet it dare not become captive to its cultural surroundings, thereby coming under the control of class and caste structures and

38

norms, or the values of a dominant ideology.

We also have to take account of the extent to which many of the forms and patterns of ministry we have inherited, as described for example by Sundkler in regard to the ministry in Africa, which are often regarded as sacrosanct, are the product of social forces rather than faithfulness to the gospel. The same question would need to be asked of any changes in form and structure which may be proposed. In so far as forms of ministry are and must be culturally related, they are sociologically determined. But some forms of ministry which have developed in the course of the centuries have been more sociologically than theologically determined, and have become encased within a tough structure which prevents urgently required change and impedes the renewal and mission of the church.[28] The substantive issue is whether the structures or forms of the ordained ministry enable or hinder it in fulfilling its task within the life of the church.

With these warnings in mind, we nevertheless have to take contextuality seriously, and affirm the vital connection between the ordained ministry and a local community of faith. In doing so we affirm the commitment of the ordained minister to a particular group of people in their hopes and struggles, their fears, doubts and failures. The call by a particular community of faith to minister in their midst should be more than a matter of form and church order; it is a commitment to that people to serve them in the name of Christ. By way of illustration, this means in the South African context that ministry has to be related to the struggles of the black community for justice and liberation, and at the same time to the fears and failures of the white community. It is the same gospel that is proclaimed, the same Christ crucified that is preached, the same call to faith and obedience that is announced, and yet the message of the gospel is addressed and expressed in different yet complementary ways.

The pastor within a black church may have to focus on the struggle for human dignity, the empowerment of people to affirm their freedom in Jesus Christ, on faith not as a way of escape from suffering but as a resource for overcoming its cause. The pastor within a white church may have to focus on the fears which people have and the way in which the gospel of Jesus Christ addresses their anxiety, on repentance for racism and the confession of guilt, on faith not as a way of escape from social responsibility but as commitment to following Jesus Christ as Lord and sharing in the struggle for just social change. Both will have to affirm the gospel of salvation and hope in Jesus Christ, and yet, as *The Kairos Document* so powerfully articulates, the message of hope will have to be expressed in different terms, terms appropriate to their different situations as white and black, affluent and poor, oppressor and oppressed.[29] *In order to do this, to fulfil the vocation of ministry, the pastor has to be a practical theologian who is able to discern the meaning of the gospel within the particular context of his or her ministry.*

The Pastor as Practical Theologian

In Germany the title 'theologian' refers in the first place not to the academic theologian but to the pastor. It is the primary designation within the Protestant churches of an ordained minister. Yet few priests or pastors would regard themselves as such, especially within the Anglo-Saxon world. In his book *Ferment in the Ministry*, the north American pastoral psychologist Seward Hiltner imagined the possible responses which ordained ministers would give to a Gallup Poll which asked the question: 'Do you regard yourself as a theologian?'

31% said, 'Well, I am a minister, but you could hardly call me a theologian.'

22% said, 'It is true I have studied theology, but I am not really a theologian.'

17% replied, 'Brother, I sure ain't. I'm only a simple parson, not one of those highpowered book guys.'

8% admitted, 'Well, I guess I am, in a way, but I am more interested in serving people than in theology.'

7% said, 'Where did you get that idea? And don't do it again.'

4% replied, 'I am about twice a year, when I go back to the alumni lectures.'

2% said, 'Pardon me, I have to rush to a funeral.'

1% snorted, 'I wonder who thought up that question?'

0.9% said, 'Yes.'[30]

Why is there this reluctance on the part of ordained ministers, to regard themselves as theologians, and, on the part of some, especially Anglo-Saxons and their heirs, why is there such antipathy towards theology? In the Germanic world the traditional tendency and temptation is precisely the opposite, to glory in the title 'theologian', and to create theologies remote from Christian praxis and existence in the world. Helmut Thielicke has a German audience in mind when, in his *A Little Exercise for Young Theologians*, he writes about the 'pathology of the young theologian's conceit'.[31] Yet even in Germany the idea that the ordained minister's self-perception is that of a theologian cannot be assumed. At Christmas in 1939 Dietrich Bonhoeffer wrote in a letter to his former students:

How superficial and flippant, especially of theologians, to send theology to the knacker's yard, to make out that one is not a theologian and doesn't want to be, and in so doing to ridicule one's own ministry and ordination and in the end to have, and to advocate, a bad theology instead of a good one![32]

This attitude parallels the tendency within the church generally to disparage theology in the interests of 'practical Christianity'.

Theology has a bad name amongst many theological students and ordained ministers, not primarily because of their modesty but because they fail to grasp its vital necessity and relevance to their vocation. Indeed, they may even regard it as something detrimental to their calling and the life and mission of the church. There are theological students who regard the study of theology as an unfortunate requirement for ordination, rather than as that which should provide the focus for their work. The image of a theologian is academic, intellectual, and far-removed from the everyday tasks of the parish minister. Much of the blame for this must be laid at the door of university departments of theology, theological colleges and seminaries, and those of us who teach in them. Theology has too often been taught in ways which reduce it to idealistic abstractions, and result in its rejection as a useful, indeed, essential part of the mission of the church and therefore of the ordained ministry. After all, the value of theology taught as a series of independent academic disciplines lacking both coherence or direction and unrelated to biblical vision or faith, is not self-evident for the Christian community struggling to be faithful in the midst of the world. This situation needs to be radically transformed if theology is to become the vocation of the ordained minister, and central to the total ministry of the

42

church, and not simply be regarded as the peculiar province of scholars.

In John T. McNeill's magnificent *A History of the Cure of Souls*, there is what we might call a 'give-away' comment which reinforces my argument that the ordained minister, is primarily a theologian. McNeill refers to the fact that 'Jean Daniel Benoit, the expert on Calvin's work in the cure of souls, states boldly that the Genevan Reformer was more a pastor than theologian', but he then continues, 'to be exact, he was a theologian in order to be a better pastor.'[33] Conversely, in his introduction to Karl Barth's essays, *Against the Stream*, Alec Vidler has this perceptive comment about the theologian's theologian, Karl Barth: 'I was aware of a quality or style about him which is hard to define. It may perhaps best be called *pastoral*, so long as this is not understood as a limitation.'[34] Christian pastors are called to be theologians, and those whom we normally designate theologians may well be pastors.

In order to describe the theological vocation and task of the ordained ministry, it is necessary to look at what we mean by theology and to distinguish between the academic theologian, the pastor as practical theologian (there are, of course, academic theologians whose discipline is practical theology), and the lay theologian. In a recent volume of essays, *The Vocation of the Theologian*, each of the nine distinguished contributors provides a different definition of theology and differing accounts of the task and methodology of the theologian. For most of them it would appear that by theologian they mean the professional academic or seminary teacher rather than the ordained minister or lay person.[35] But the title theologian can be applied equally to all three, academic, ordained minister and lay person, as long as we keep certain distinctions in mind. 'Theological *responsibility* is' as Nicholas Lash reminds us, 'ineluctably

43

borne by every Christian individual and by all Christian groups and institutions.'[36] But their tasks, though always complementary, are often different.

The differences arise from the nature of theology, the way in which it has developed over the centuries, and the different arenas, or what David Tracy calls 'publics', within which theology occurs: the university, the community of faith, and the public sphere.[37] Each of these has its own language of discourse and criteria for evaluating what is said and done. For example, within the academy or university the theologian is engaged in a scientific task alongside other disciplines where rationality is the norm. Within the church the focus of theology is upon the confession of faith and witness of the community of faith in the world. I would not wish to push these distinctions too far, however. The academic 'public' remains part of the body politic, after all, and it is impossible to separate the academic theologian from the community of faith and its witness.

As an 'academic theologian', I believe in the importance of teaching and doing theology within an academic context. Nicholas Lash, in speaking of the responsibilities of the academic theologian in relation to the church, puts it sharply when he writes that 'if the Christian community is really concerned with truth, rather than with reassurance, then it should demand of its academics that they be fearless in enquiry and quite uncompromisingly rigorous in their stands of exploration and argument.' In parenthesis he continues, 'It should also, I might add, be tolerant of the technicality that is frequently inseparable from such rigour.'[38] In the Foreword to the first volume of his *Church Dogmatics*, Karl Barth responds to those who might question the relevance of such an enterprise in Germany in 1932 by saying that it is precisely in such times that the church needs to clarify its faith as comprehensively as possible.

I believe as a matter of fact that a better Church dogmatics (even apart from all utilitarian ethical applications) might be an ultimately weightier and more solid contribution even to questions and tasks like that of German liberation, than most of the well-meant stuff which so many, even among theologians, think in their dilettantism they should and can supply, with respect to these questions and tasks.[39]

This rings important bells for those of us who do theology in the South African situation.

Yet, it is clear that doing theology within the sphere of the university is different in many ways from doing it within the community of faith engaged in mission. It is also different from doing theology in the context of a theological seminary. There is within the academic community, to return to David Tracy's term, a different 'public' with which the theologian is in discussion. The primary concern of the pastor as practical theologian in the community of faith is not academic discourse, but the confession or witness of the church in the world. A confession which, in some situations like my own, requires the capacity to declare certain theogies a heresy. There is, thus, always a tension between theology as it is pursued within the academy and the church. But they also need each other.

Academic theology must not become a closed, abstract system out of touch with concrete reality and unrelated to those who are seeking to confess their faith in God within the world. If it does this it simply becomes a branch of philosophy. On the other hand, the confessing theology of a community of faith can so easily become ghetto-theology if it is cut off from the rigorous and critical scrutiny of academic theological endeavour. Reflecting on the state of theology in Britain and especially its captivity to the middle and upper-middle class, Jose Miguez-Bonino, the Argentinian liberation theologian, has said that while 'one of the

45

basic problems for theology' is 'how to relate the theological enterprise actively to the large Christian community and to society as a whole', 'this does not mean (we must caution against a false conclusion that has already caused some damage in our own situation) a lessening of scholarly concern or disregard for the academic community.' But Miguez-Bonino goes on to say that 'it does mean that unless theology finds a way to overcome class captivity, it cannot expect to render a true service to the "whole people of God", either within the Churches or in the wider social body.'[40]

In the South African situation, as elsewhere, ordained ministers, at least within the mainline churches, are academically trained and may be regarded as part of the elite. What I am pleading for is, however, not the perpetuation of such a division within the life of the church and the wider community. For what I regard as the theological vocation of the ordained ministry applies equally, for example, to unschooled bishops within the African indigenous churches as it does to academically trained pastors and priests within the mainline churches. Which brings us back to our definition of the practical theologian as one who provides leadership and direction for the community of faith.

Drawing on recent thinking in management theory, Hough and Cobb suggest the designation of 'pathfinder' for their model of the practical theologian.

> Pathfinders are persons with a vision of what the institution is to become, of where it ought to be in the future. They are persons with passionate commitments, able to inspire others to share their commitments. . . . Church members expect their leaders to be something more than problem-solvers and implementers. They expect them to be able to give guidance to their own reflection about who Christians

are and what this Christian identity implies for their living practice in the world.[41]

Karl Rahner defines practical theology in a way very similar to this, and thereby enables us to correlate leadership within the community of faith with the role of the priest or pastor. 'Practical theology' he writes, 'is that theological discipline which is concerned with the Church's self-actualisation here and now – both that which *is* and that which *ought to be*.'[42] Amongst other things, this means that the ordained ministry has to be adequately trained in the historical tradition of Christian faith, and especially its Biblical foundations, because it is precisely this which enables the church to maintain its identity and fulfil its unique task in the present context. 'What the church needs now' write Hough and Cobb, 'is leadership in recovering its internal history so that its identity in the world as the church is strengthened and clarified.'[43] To return to Sundkler's phrase regarding the emerging model of the ordained ministry in Africa, the church needs representative leadership.

The primary task of the ministry of the Word and Sacraments is to enable the upbuilding of the church *in such a way* that it is always pointed beyond itself to the reign of God in Jesus Christ in the midst of the world. Its task is to keep the People of God mindful of the tradition of Jesus, crucified and risen, and what this means for their lives and the praxis of the church today. Its task is to enable the church to be faithful to its identity as the People of God in the world, discerning who God is and what God requires of them. In this way the ministry of the Word and Sacraments is, literally-speaking, church leadership because it provides theological direction for the mission of the People of God in the world.

Practical Theology and the Knowledge of God

In some notes on theology and the Christian community ('Theologie und Gemeinde') which he probably drafted in 1940, Dietrich Bonhoeffer provides us with important preliminary insights in regard to the place of theology in the life of the church. Having referred to the various ways in which theology is understood, or misunderstood, he reminds us that 'the essence of the Christian community is not to pursue theology, but to believe and obey the Word of God.' Yet he goes on to say that the proclamation of this Word is open to all kinds of falsification simply because it is proclaimed by humans in human words. Hence the need for theology, not as a replacement for faith, nor as a substitute for proclamation, and certainly not as 'an end in itself', but as 'a resource and a weapon'.[44]

Theology, Bonhoeffer argues, is a human, critical task through which the Christian church is reminded of the meaning of Biblical faith, the history of that faith in Christian tradition and its confessions, and its contemporary meaning. In this way theology contributes a vital dimension to the struggle for truth and faithfulness in the present. Faith and discipleship are not primarily something intellectual; they have to do with existential commitment in response to the mystery of grace. In Bonhoeffer's terms, they belong to the category of *actus directus*, rather than to *actus reflectus* which is the essence of theology as human, critical reflection.[45]

Keeping these distinctions in mind, let us further clarify what is meant by theology, and especially practical theology, by considering Edward Farley's recent discussion of the history of the concept *theologia*. Farley maintains that the reason why the term 'theology' is so ambiguous and unclear today, derives from the fact that even in premodern times it was used to refer 'to things of entirely different *genres*'.

> First, theology is a term for an actual, individual cognition of God and things related to God, a cognition which in most treatments attends faith and has eternal happiness as its final goal. Second, theology is a term for a discipline, a self-conscious scholarly enterprise of understanding. In the former sense theology is a habit (*habitus*) of the human soul. In the latter it is a discipline, usually occurring in some sort of pedagogical setting. The ambiguity, the double reference and genre of the term *theology* does not originate with theology itself, the church and its teachers. It is the outcome of a similar ambiguity and double reference occurring in the language of human 'science' in premodern Western philosophy.[46]

Farley traces the historical development of theology in terms of these two different uses of the concept, both of which have their own history, and both of which are equally important. But he then shows how, largely under the impact of the eighteenth century Enlightenment, both understandings of theology became radically distorted, thus creating a major crisis for theology in our time.

> Theology as a personal quality continues (though not usually under the term *theology*), not as a salvation-disposed wisdom, but as the practical know-how necessary to ministerial work. Theology as discipline continues, not as the unitary enterprise of theological study, but as one technical and specialized scholarly undertaking among others; in other words, as systematic theology.[47]

Thus theology as that which has to do with a living, redemptive knowledge of God, and theology as that integrative discipline which enables faith in God to understand itself, have virtually been lost in a multitude of disciplines, only one of which is normally labelled theology.

The study of theology can, and probably must be subdivided. The traditional distinctions are normally, as David Tracy reminds us, between fundamental, systematic and practical theology. *Fundamental theology* deals with foundational questions of faith at a relatively abstract level; *systematic theology* is the interpretation of the Christian tradition in and for a particular situation; *practical theology* is the interface between the tradition and concrete engagement in the life of the world (praxis), in which critical theory and praxis are in a mutually critical relationship.[48] Any failure to recognise these distinctions leads to confusion and misunderstanding both with regard to the nature of theology and the theological task of the ordained minister. And yet, just as doing theology in the academy, the church and the wider society are all interrelated, so too, it is necessary and important to recognise the interrelatedness and interdependency of fundamental, systematic and practical theology. They may be undertaken by different people within different 'publics' but they are interdependent. The pastor, as practical theologian, like the academic practical theologian, should also be concerned about fundamental and systematic theology, because these disciplines provide grounding in the tradition and necessary insight for the task of critical reflection on ecclesial praxis.

In the historical process to which Farley refers, however, practical theology becomes one amongst other disciplines in the theological curriculum, but not an integral part of theology as such. It is reduced to a 'know-how' subject, applied theology, in which the pastor seeks to apply theory to the tasks or praxis of ministry. Thus the practical theologian becomes the ecclesiastical technician, while the academic theologian is caught up in his or her speciality and more often than not in questions of method rather than the constructive task of providing theological insight and direction for today.[49] No wonder the poor student of theology, anticipating a pastoral future is not sure why theology has to be studied or endured. Theology understood both as *habitus*, and theology as that scientific discipline which seeks to provide us with an integrated understanding of faith, the Christian tradition, and a holistic vision of reality has largely disappeared.

Gustavo Gutierrez in *A Theology of Liberation* makes a similar distinction to that made by Farley. He refers to 'theology as wisdom', an understanding rooted both in Scripture and Patristic theology, and one which remains fundamental to Eastern Orthodoxy, and 'theology as rational knowledge'. The latter developed particularly from the twelfth century, reaching its apex in Thomas Aquinas and Catholic Scholasticism. Both of them, Gutierrez rightly maintains, constitute permanent dimensions of theology, and must be included within the theological enterprise, although it is not always apparent that Gutierrez does this himself.

However, there is a third understanding of theology, theology as critical reflection on the social praxis of the church, which Gutierrez makes the focal point for doing theology today. This approach is fundamental to all contemporary theologies of liberation and it adds a critical, socio-political dimension which is missing in Farley's approach. Hough and Cobb rightly 'fear that Farley's *theologia* would so focus on personal and ecclesial life as to distract attention from the historical horizons of the world God loves'.[50] Methodologically, as Gutierrez claims, liberation theology goes back to the early centuries of Christianity, finding expression above all in St Augustine's *City of God*, where theology has to do with the understanding of God in relation to our historical context.[51] In its contemporary form, as a theology of social critique and

51

transformation, it radically challenges the very way in which theology has usually been done in the past. As such, it is doing theology in the prophetic tradition of the eighth century B.C. Hebrew prophets.

On the basis of our discussion, but also in anticipation of what follows, I propose that theology be understood, firstly, in a holistic, integrated way in which the various disciplines (biblical studies, church history, fundamental, systematic and practical theology) are regarded as integral parts of the same theological task. These theological disciplines also need to be in a critical but integral relationship with other disciplines, especially the social sciences. Secondly, that we retain the original meaning of theology as having to do with the 'knowledge of God', a knowledge grasped by faith in Jesus Christ witnessed to in the Scriptures. Theology cannot be equated with that knowledge; but it is the necessary human attempt to understand and clarify what it means. Thirdly, theology is concerned with what it means 'to know God' in relation to our human existence within a specific historical context. While this is intensely personal and ecclesial, it also has to do with social justice and transformation. Fourthly, the task of theology is the retrieval of those symbols within Christian tradition, their critique and restatement, which communicate the transformative power and vision of the gospel. Thus, theology is critical reflection on the church's confession of faith and social praxis in the light of the Word of God in order that we might better know and serve God revealed in Jesus Christ today.

The theological basis for such an understanding of the task of theology is the doctrine of the Incarnation and the conviction that in Jesus Christ the kingdom of God has broken into our history thereby opening it up for God's transforming action in a new and decisive way. The Word of God which enables us to 'know God' becomes part of our human and historical context in Jesus of Nazareth. His life, fate, and victory within first century Palestine are crucial for our understanding of God today, and our participation as the People of God in the *missio Dei*. The witness to him in Scripture, and to the prophetic tradition in which he stood, are thus fundamental to critical reflection on our own faith and obedience, including the struggle for justice, liberation and peace. At several places in the chapters which follow we shall develop some of these themes further. For the moment let us look at two different ways in which the Incarnation has been dealt with in recent theological study in order to illustrate the point we are making.

In several of the essays in Rex Ambler and David Haslam's *Agenda for Prophets* there is reference to the debate occasioned in English theology by the publication of John Hick's *The Myth of God Incarnate*. On each occasion the observation is made that the debate has to do with the problem of believing in and understanding the Incarnation rather than with its implications for the life and witness of the church in the world. Clearly the doctrine of the Incarnation, like any other article of Christian faith, must be subject to critical reflection and study, and it would be shortsighted of the church to try and prevent such investigations. Hick's concern is a legitimate one, and while we may not agree with his conclusions, we have to wrestle with his argument. At one level, then, the 'myth debate' Hick engendered is relevant to the challenge facing the church in the world because it has to do with the meaning of Jesus Christ for us today. At another level the debate is abstruse, somewhat academic and removed from the real struggles of the practical theologian and the witness of the church.

Compare the 'myth debate' in Britain and elsewhere in the first world to what we find in the writings of so-called third world theologians. As an example, take Frank Chikane's essay 'The Incarnation in the Life of the People in Southern Africa' which he gave in 1985, a few months before his arrest on a charge of high treason.[52] Chikane began his address by strongly affirming the Incarnation as fundamental for Christian faith: Jesus Christ is truly God become fully human. On that basis, which is admittedly an article of faith and not one of scientific proof, Chikane then examined the ways in which the Incarnation has been understood within Western theology. He concludes that in the process, and under the influence of Western philosophy, the divinity and humanity of Jesus have been torn apart with disastrous consequences for the church and its mission.

Chikane does not simply wish to restate Chalcedonian Christology, but, in a way reminiscent of Bonhoeffer's *Christology*, he regards that as clearing the ground for the statement of who Jesus Christ is for us today. The important question is not 'how' the Incarnation is possible, but 'who' the Incarnate One is.[53] In order to get at that question, Chikane, like other liberation and third world theologians, begins with Jesus of Nazareth and the proclamation of the kingdom of God. Jesus not only enables us to see that God becomes known within specific historical contexts, but, in fact, defines who God is and what it means to 'know God'.[54] Thus the doctrine of the Incarnation is set free from abstract categories and becomes the explosive centre of theology within our own historical reality. It makes it possible for us to grasp the content of that revelation in a way that directly relates to our own specific situation.

Just as the ministry is essentially part of the doctrine of the church, so the church is part of Christology. Everything finds its focus in Jesus Christ, the Word of God. The point of departure for Christian theology, including practical theology, is the question, as Bonhoeffer rightly perceived,

'Who is Jesus Christ, for us, today?' In other words, the real theological task is not to prove the existence of God, for that must ultimately be a matter of faith, but to enable the community of faith critically to understand its faith and express answers to the questions: *who* is God, *where* is God to be found today, and what does *this* God require of us *here and now*? The academic theologian may well provide resources for answering these questions. But it is the practical theologian within the community of faith who has to help the community day by day and week by week discover the answers in relation to the praxis and witness of the church in the world, and so help it find the direction which enables it to be faithful to its task.

Theology as a Gift of the Spirit

Earlier I referred to the antipathy which many theological students and ordained ministers have with regard to the study of theology and to the designation theologian. Quite apart from this antipathy, however, there is also a reluctance to regard oneself as a theologian which derives from a genuine and appropriate sense of inadequacy. Theologians need to keep in mind the frequent warnings of Jesus against the teachers of the law of his day. 'Theologian', is, after all, a lofty title for any human being to claim. In the *Preface to his German Writings*, Martin Luther had this to say about the proud theologian:

> If you feel and are inclined to think you have made it, flattering yourself with your own little books, teaching or writing, because you have done it beautifully and preached excellently; if you are highly pleased when someone praises you in the presence of others; if perhaps you look for praise,

and would sulk or quit what you are doing if you did not get it – if you are of that stripe, dear friend, then take yourself by the ears, and if you do this in the right way you will find a beautiful pair of big, long, shaggy donkey ears. Then do not spare any expense! Decorate them with golden bells, so that people will be able to hear you wherever you go, point their fingers at you, and say, 'See, See! There goes that clever beast, who can write such exquisite books and preach so remarkably well.' That very moment you will be blessed and blessed beyond measure in the kingdom of heaven. Yes, in that heaven where hellfire is ready for the devil and his angels.[55]

In his masterful introduction to *Evangelical Theology*, Karl Barth thus asks of himself and of us:

After all, who am I to be a theologian? . . . Who am I to have put such trust in myself as to devote myself even remotely to the task of theology? Who am I to co-operate in this subject, at least potentially and perhaps quite actively, as a minor researcher, thinker or teacher? Who am I to take up the quest for truth in the service and in the sense of the community, and to take pains to complete this quest.[56]

All true theology begins and ends humbly and modestly. For the Christian, as Luther so powerfully stated in the 'Heidelberg Disputation' (article 20), it begins at the cross. 'He deserves to be called a theologian' Luther wrote, 'who comprehends the visible and manifest things of God seen through suffering and the cross.'[57] Bonhoeffer was attracted to Georges Bernanos' portraits of priests in his books because, as Bonhoeffer wrote: 'When priests speak in them, their words carry weight. The reason is that they are not products of some sort of verbalised reflection of observation but quite simply of daily, personal intercourse with the crucified Jesus Christ. These are the depths from which a word must come if it is to carry weight.'[58]

However, while the perspective and attitude of the theologian should be shaped by the suffering servanthood of Jesus Christ, there is no way we can relinquish the task. Nor need we relinquish the title of theologian. Rather we should see it not as something which has to do with our own skills and training, but as a calling and a gift of the Spirit, one of the gifts necessary for the ministry and mission of the church. Paul Tillich, in a sermon to seminarians entitled 'The Theologian' put this with characteristic perception:

> What makes a man a theologian? What is his relation to other forms of existence? What is the significance of our existence as a whole? Paul makes very clear what he thinks is the foundation of all theology: the Divine Spirit. And the word of wisdom and knowledge, theology, according to the witness of the whole Christian Church, is basically a gift of the Spirit. It is *one* of the gifts, besides others. It is a *special* gift, besides other special gifts. But it is a *gift* of the Spirit, and not a natural capacity. The word of knowledge – theology – is spoken to *us* before *we* can say it to others, or even to ourselves. To be a theologian means first of all to be able to *receive* spiritual knowledge.[59]

To be a theologian is a vocation, it is, in Pauline language, a charism before it becomes an institutional office. This applies not just in the history of the development of the ordained ministry, but also in the case of each person who is called to this ministry. The leadership of which we speak is, as Sundkler discerned, not only representative leadership but also charismatic.

Although theology has to do with the Word of God that comes to us in Jesus Christ to whom the Scriptures bear witness, it remains nonetheless a human enterprise, not least because it has to do with the meaning of the Incarnate Word in changing historical contexts. Such knowledge does not drop from the sky; it arises out of the often agonising and always fallible human struggle to know who Jesus Christ is for us today in our own situation and, therefore, what God requires of us here and now. This is why the vocation of the ordained minister is such a threatening and audacious task. 'As ministers we ought to speak of God,' wrote Karl Barth. 'We are human, however, and so we cannot speak of God. We ought therefore to recognise both *our obligation* and *our inability* and by that very recognition give God the glory. This is our perplexity. The rest of the our task fades into insignificance in comparison.'[60] In such matters 'even the "expert",' Lash reminds us, 'is necessarily an "amateur",' for, 'there are not, nor can there ever be, "experts" in the knowledge of God: not even the saints, let alone the scholars.'[61]

An audacious, frightening and daunting task, the theological task of the ordained minister remains, nonetheless, an essential one that must be pursued. Otherwise we must admit immediately that there is no Word for us today, no meaning in the universe of which we are part, no direction for the community of faith and the struggle for justice, because there is no hope, only silence, emptiness, the void. The theologian, struggling often with an intense sense of inadequacy, plagued perhaps by doubts, nevertheless seeks to discern and proclaim the Word of God, not as a Word that by-passes the agonies of life and its struggles against evil, but as a Word which speaks to the human condition from the cross. The theologian does not have superior knowledge which enables him or her to see things *sub species aeternitas*, but committed to the God become flesh, the God incarnate in Jesus of Nazareth, the theologian simply seeks to bear witness to the crucified Christ as Lord here and now.

To return to St John the 'Golden Mouth' and Richard Baxter, with whom we began this chapter. Both were preeminently practical theologians; both put a great premium on preaching, indeed on expository preaching; both were prolific writers; and both were so involved in the affairs of their tumultuous times as servants of the gospel that they ran foul of the authorities, both, it may be mentioned, being rather undiplomatic in their approach to those in power. Twice banished from his see, Chrysostom finally died a slow martyr's death on a forced march in severe winter weather; for thirty years Baxter was banned by the authorities from preaching, abused, persecuted and finally imprisoned for his defence of nonconformity.

Yet, there is something else which relates them. Chrysostom's ideal priest and Baxter's reformed pastor are, above all else, committed to Jesus Christ in such a way that both their affections and their minds were brought together in the service of the gospel. That, I would suggest, is the primary description of a theologian. Someone who is so committed to Jesus Christ and the service of the gospel that there is no false dualism, no dichotomy, which separates his or her commitment into separate spheres, no sundering of the personal and the political, no cleavage between the public arena, the study and the pulpit. When Hugh Martin refers to Baxter's 'breadth of outlook, his scholarship, his passion for social justice and his zeal for the honour, purity and unity of Christ's Church',[62] he provides us with a model of a true theologian which we may well wish to emulate.

Thomas Long rightly perceives that 'before ministry is a way of *doing*, it is a way of *seeing, knowing,* and *believing.* Ministry is a task, but it grows out of a gift of vision.' He continues, 'ministry which operates apart from that vision finally dissolves into technique.'[63] At all costs we must avoid reducing theology to a technique; what we are concerned about is ultimately theology as a vision, a vision of God in relation to the transformation of the world and our lives. It is for this reason that the Eastern Orthodox tradition defines a theologian preeminently as a person of prayer, that is, a person who lives in relationship with God and so discerns God's will and becomes part of God's gracious transforming action. But this is not confined to the Orthodox tradition, it is universally recognised. Writing of Julian of Norwich, A.M. Allchin remarks that 'a theologian is one whose prayer is true; one whose prayer is true is a theologian.'[64] Consider also how Karl Barth in his lectures on *Evangelical Theology* spoke of prayer as the 'first and basic act' of theology.

> Any theology which would not even consider the necessity to respond to God personally could only be a false theology. It would exchange what is real for what is unreal if it did not unfailingly keep sight of this I-Thou relationship in which God is man's God and man is God's man. Implicitly and explicitly, proper theology will have to be *Proslogion*, *Suspirium*, or prayer. It will meditate on the fact that God can be its object only because he is the acting and speaking subject upon whom all depends.[65]

CHAPTER TWO

Theology, Prophecy, and Pastoral Practice

Towards the end of 1985 a group of theologians and pastors in South Africa, who live and work in the black townships around Johannesburg, produced 'The Kairos Document: A Theological Comment on the Political Crisis in South Africa.' South African churches and theologians have issued many statements criticising apartheid since its increasingly rigid enforcement in 1948. These statements have reflected a liberal concern for racial justice, and have been critical of the state ideology with its Christian pretensions. They have understood themselves as representing the biblical prophetic tradition and witnessing to the kingdom of God. In the name of prophetic theology, however, the 'Kairos theologians', not only rejected what they called 'state theology' ('the theological justification' by the state 'of the status quo with its racism, capitalism and totalitarianism'), but were also critical of 'church theology'. This theology, they argued, is reflected in the statements of church leaders whose criticism of apartheid 'is superficial and counter-productive'. Over against both 'state' and 'church theology', they declared:

> Our present KAIROS calls for a response from Christians that is biblical, spiritual, pastoral and, above all, prophetic. It is not enough in these circumstances to repeat generalised Christian principles. We need a bold and incisive response that is prophetic because it speaks to the particular circumstances of this crisis, a response that does not give the impression of sitting on the fence but is clearly and unambiguously taking a stand.[1]

61

A prophetic response – but one which is pastoral.

If asked, Christian social activists, participants in the charismatic renewal movement, and Seventh Day Adventists, to mention no others, would define biblical prophecy in very different, even contradictory ways. They would certainly not all agree with the Kairos theologians' interpretation. One reason for this is that all of us read Scripture through our own ideological and theological spectacles, and therefore tend to see in it what we wish to find. But another important reason is that prophecy in the Bible, both in the Old and New Testaments, is a very complex phenomenon which lends itself to a variety of interpretations.[2] Prophecy is understood and engaged in differently within both the Old and the New Testaments. Thus, in his book *Prophecy and Praxis* Robin Gill cautions that 'if Christians are to use the Old Testament prophetic tradition today, they cannot assume that it presents a single or consistent critique of society.'[3] Stanley Hauerwas spells this out more fully:

> one cannot assume that the current understanding of 'prophetic' is in fact synonymous with the role of the prophets in the Hebrew scriptures. For example, the prophets are often treated as social radicals who were willing to overthrow their social order in the interests of justice. Yet one is increasingly aware that many of the prophets were profound social conservatives who were seeking not to overthrow the status quo, but to maintain it, or even to return to a prior way of life.[4]

To refer, then, to 'the prophetic tradition' as though its meaning is self-evident to all and beyond the realm of debate, will not do. Like 'the Kairos theologians' we have to be much more specific and indicate as precisely as possible what we do mean, and therefore what we also intend when we speak of prophecy. And as our focus is upon the ordained minister as practical theologian, we will need to consider how prophecy relates to theology and to the responsibilities of the priest and pastor.

Theology and the Prophetic Tradition

Walter Brueggemann has shown that within the Old Testament there are two trajectories or traditions arising out of the covenant, the one derived from Moses and the other being Davidic in its formulation.[5] Both trajectories have their theologians and prophets. In the Davidic tradition, or the Royal trajectory, the prophets are supportive of the monarchy and urban privileged classes, the religious hierarchy and cultus and, especially in post-exilic Israel they are also nationalists committed to the purity of Judaism. The theology of these prophets is expressed in the 'myths of unity', their interest is that of creation and the continuity of institutions, and their 'preferred mode of perception is that of universal comprehensiveness'. In the Mosaic tradition, or what Brueggemann refers to as the 'liberation trajectory', the focus is on God's justice and righteousness, a concern for the poor and the peasants and, therefore, a commitment to social transformation and the establishment of an egalitarian society. Their 'preferred mode of perception is that of historical specificity', their language is historically concrete and focusses on 'stories of liberation'.[6] Once again we encounter the tension between universality and contextuality.

It is beyond the scope of what we are attempting to debate the details of Brueggemann's thesis, and especially the extent to which the two trajectories are complementary or

63

mutually exclusive. But in broad outline I wish to affirm the position he adopts, and to follow him in the perceptive way in which he uses these trajectories to 'illuminate the various alternatives in current theological discussion'. For this purpose he distinguishes between two main types of theology which he refers to as 'process hermeneutics and liberation hermeneutics'. 'Process theologies', as I understand his argument, does not necessarily refer to what is commonly called Process Theology, but is an umbrella term for theologies which share certain similarities. He describes them as follows:

> Process theologies may be generally placed in the trajectory of royal theology which is concerned with large comprehensive issues, which regards the concreteness of historical memory as a matter of little interest, and which is concerned with the continuities of the process. Current scholarly investigation within this trajectory: (a) is likely seeking meaningful interface with current cultural forms; (b) is most likely to be lodged in university contexts and their epistemological commitments and not primarily interested in the forming of the synagogue/church as an alternative and distinct community of faith; and (c) is likely to have an inherent bias towards social conservatism.

'Conversely', Brueggemann goes on to say, 'the various liberation theologies in their epistemological abrasiveness likely may be located on the trajectory rooted in Moses.'

> They are inclined to focus on the concreteness of historical memory and regard more sweeping, unitive statements as less important and compelling. Current scholarly work in this trajectory: (a) is likely not so directly concerned with contact with cultural forms and values but is addressed to a particular faith community living in uneasy tension with the dominant cultural forms and values; (b) is most likely to be lodged in a confessing community or school of it. It is

64

inclined to be concerned primarily with the faithful effectiveness of the confessing community and to believe that the dominant rationality will permit no ready point of contact without coopting. And, if the scholar is lodged in a university context, it is still likely the case that the main referent is a confessing group; (c) is likely to have an intrinsic bias toward social ethical radicalness.[7]

The strong and stark contrasts which Brueggemann draws between these two types of theology may need to be qualified in different ways, as he himself recognises. Process-type theologians may well be concerned about contextual issues and radical social action, and liberation-type theologians may also have a concern for culture, universality, and continuity. But Brueggemann's analysis clearly shows the interrelatedness between different types of theology and prophecy in the Old Testament and in our own time.

Time and again in the history of Christianity theology has been misused to legitimate ecclesiastical and theological triumphalism, and to sanctify the power of the state. This is one reason why so-called 'theologies from above' have become suspect by those Christians engaged in the struggle for social justice and liberation. They are too often theologies of alienation which produce a false consciousness both amongst those with power and the powerless. In fact, such theologies reflect the ideology of those in power, those who rule from above, and thereby reinforce structures of domination. They are the theologies of the court theologians and prophets which serve the interests of the state and the cultus. They are theologies of uncritical patriotism, theologies which are not committed to hearing the living Word of the Lord today in our present crisis and context.

The focus of prophetic theology remains that of theology as a whole, namely, the knowledge of God. But in its critical reflection on social praxis it seeks to counter false claims to such knowledge, to expose false prophecy and the theology which underlies and supports it. Because theologians themselves, and that includes ordained ministers, can so easily become seduced by such alienation, prophetic theology understood as critical reflection on praxis can also set theologians free, leading them 'to discover elements of false consciousness in their perception of reality and thus produce a significant change of mind and heart'.[8] Thus prophetic theology is not simply addressed to the powers, it is also addressed to pastors and preachers, to the prophets themselves.

Critical theology as such, however, is not prophecy, it is always, as Gutierrez says, 'the second step', that reflective task which follows prophecy and praxis.[9] To return to Bonhoeffer's distinction, it is *actus reflectus* rather than *actus directus*. The task of the practical theologian is to reflect critically on ecclesial and social praxis in the light of the biblical, liberatory tradition within his or her particular context. And yet, as we shall see more fully in the next chapter, because hermeneutics is always a circular process in which reflection not only follows action but also precedes the next moment of engagement, critical or prophetic theology is that theology which enables prophecy to flourish in continuity with the transformative vision of the liberatory tradition.

For the Kairos theologians a prophetic theology is thus one which is critical of theologies, whether of the state or church, which legitimate or help to perpetuate an unjust social system. It is equally one which unambiguously takes the side of the oppressed and serves the cause of justice and liberation. It is theology in the Mosaic tradition of the eighth to sixth century Hebrew prophets who were engaged in radical social analysis and critique, rhetoric and dissent, and who were committed to a vision of society which required fundamental social transformation. The question we now have to ask is whether there is any continuity between this prophetic tradition and prophecy in the church as it is portrayed in the New Testament? And, if so, how does it relate to the theological task of the leadership of the Christian church, and pastoral practice in the life of the congregation?

The Prophetic Ministry of Jesus

Prophecy in the New Testament is as complex a phenomenon as in the Old. After an exhaustive examination of the evidence, David Aune in fact concludes that Christian prophecy in the New Testament 'does not readily lend itself to categorical conceptualisation' and that it was 'a relatively *unstable and unstructured institution within early Christianity*'.[10] Moreover, Aune indicates that only a small minority of references to prophecy in the New Testament 'refer to Old Testament type prophetic activity'.[11]

While the letter to the Ephesians tells us that the church was 'built on the foundation of the apostles and prophets' (Ephesians 2:20 NIV), it would appear that the role of the apostles rather than the prophets was the establishment of congregations in the faith and tradition of Jesus.[12] Yet the foundational role of the prophet was equally crucial. As a recognised charismatic-type leader, the prophet proclaimed the word of the living Lord to the assembled congregation in the power of the Spirit.

In the absence of the more complex bureaucratic organisation which accompanied the institutionalisation of early

67

Christianity, prophets appear to have played a more visible and active role in guiding Christian communities in decision making by reiterating the norms and values which were an integral part of Christian tradition and by providing the communities with visible evidence of the presence and activity of God and Jesus.[13]

Thus the role of the prophets, at least in Pauline-type congregations, was not that of social criticism but of witness to Jesus Christ within the body in order that the church could discern 'the mind of Christ' and be built up in faith, hope and love. They were, in fact, those leaders within the congregation who sought to articulate the tradition of Jesus in new contexts so that the word of the living Lord could be heard. The apostolic tradition and faith to be proclaimed throughout the whole world, and the prophetic Word in the Spirit to be proclaimed in a particular historical context, belonged together.

The Scriptures of the New Testament are the product of precisely this process of interplay between prophetic Word and theological reflection, as well as between universal significance and contextual concern. Each of the four gospels is addressed to a particular audience, Mark to the Christian community in Rome, for example, at a time of social uncertainty and political crisis. Similarly the epistles of Paul and the other letter writers have specific contexts in mind. While the Book of the Revelation, with its letters to the seven churches in which the Spirit of Jesus addresses the congregations by the prophet according to their peculiar circumstances, and yet does so against the background of the cosmic drama of God's redemption, is a prime example of the process.

There is, however, within the New Testament a direct continuation of the Old Testament prophetic tradition as social and cultic criticism in the life and death of Jesus of

Nazareth.[14] This comes through particularly strongly in both Matthew and Luke's portrayal of Jesus' ministry and fate, as well as in the letter of James. Although the primitive Christian community regarded Jesus as far more than a prophet, he was undoubtedly for them also a prophet, and in all probability Jesus regarded himself as a prophet in continuity with the eighth century Hebrew prophets in the Mosaic tradition.[15] Indeed, says David Hill, there is the likelihood that 'many of the characteristics of the Old Testament prophets may have been mediated to the earliest Christian prophets through Jesus' exemplification of them in speech and action.'[16]

In the history of Christian dogmatics the threefold office of Jesus as Prophet, Priest and King has had an honoured place.[17] According to this formulation Jesus fulfils in himself these three Old Testament offices, and thereby brings them to an end. Thus according to Calvin's Geneva Catechism (1541), Christ 'was the sovereign messenger and ambassador of God his Father, to give a full exposition of God's will toward the world and so put an end to all prophecies and revelations (Heb. 1:2)'.[18] A more acceptable approach, which meets Calvin's concern but does not rule out the word of prophecy for today, is that of Karl Barth. Yet Barth himself refers to the attempt to be prophetic in the Old Testament sense without reference to the gospel as false prophecy! He writes:

> We cannot fail to insist that much preaching which is well meant, and perhaps deeply sincere and moving, even having a touch of inspiration and ecstasy, but prophetic only in the Old Testament sense, is false prophecy. Nor can even the most powerful preaching of the Law in abstraction, whether directed to individual, social or political concerns, escape the same verdict.[19]

Christian witness must center on Jesus Christ as God's true

witness, and the good news of God's reconciling grace in him. Thus Christian prophecy must be Christological. The alternative is to turn the gospel into law and to reduce prophecy to moralising. We are thus back to the question raised by Bonhoeffer: 'who is Jesus Christ for us today?', a question we shall explore in detail in the next chapter, though we need to begin that exploration here.

The point of departure for the Christology of the synoptic gospels is the arrival of the reign of God in Jesus of Nazareth. The coming of Jesus is a kairos-event, a critical moment in the history of Israel and the world, long-awaited by the humble and poor, dreaded by the powerful and rich. While there is undoubtedly a predictive element in prophecy, Jesus' fulfilment of the prophets (Matthew 5:17) must surely be understood as him being in continuity with those who proclaimed the law, or Torah, against the injustice and oppression of their day. That is, Jesus stands in what Breuggemann calls the liberatory trajectory.

Jesus' controversy with the Pharisees is precisely one in which he rejects the way in which the Torah is misused to sanction the status quo and preserve those 'traditions of men' which, in the name of the Torah, deny its critical power and sanction the oppression of the poor. Jesus represents another tradition, the tradition which faithfully articulates the Torah in his own critical moment and context. Thus, according to Matthew, Jesus attacks the Pharisees with the words: 'Woe to you, teachers of the law and Pharisees, you hypocrites! You give a tenth of your spices – mint, dill and cummin. But you have neglected the more important matters of the law – justice, mercy and faithfulness' (23:23). Jesus as prophet does not deny the tradition of the Torah, he affirms it most strongly, yet he affirms it by restating and applying its demands in a new time and situation.

We are likewise familiar with the canticles in the Lukan nativity stories which stand in direct line with the prophetic tradition, and also with Jesus' own identification of his mission with the liberatory role of the prophet Messiah in Luke 4:16-21. Jesus' mission is demonstrated in his liberating praxis, his concern for the oppressed, whether they be women, the poor, or those who are deaf, dumb, blind or possessed by demons. Through his actions Jesus proclaims that the reign of God has begun in a new and decisive way, and that it is in continuity with the tradition that began with Moses and found its expression in the prophets of Israel. In other words, Jesus' ministry does not bring to an end the liberatory prophetic tradition, on the contrary, Jesus makes it central to his own mission and confirms it with his suffering, death and resurrection. In doing so, Jesus deepens and transforms the tradition, filling it with new content because in him the reign of God has broken decisively into human history.

In Jesus, then, the prophetic tradition is fulfilled and the faithful proclamation of Jesus as the Christ, as redeemer and as Lord, by the church not only can but must be in continuity with the socially critical and liberating witness of the prophets if it is to be faithful to the gospel of the kingdom of God. This does not mean reducing Jesus' status to that of teacher, as in liberal theology, or regarding him along with John the Baptist as the last of the prophets; on the contrary, *it means exalting the prophetic task as a permanent responsibility within the People of God.* Precisely because Jesus is both Messiah and Lord, the continuity of the prophetic witness becomes central to and definitive for the mission and ministry of the church. Thus the rejection of Marcionism, the attempt to excise the Old Testament and much of the New from the Christian Scriptures, by the early church was essential to the survival of the church as the church of Jesus Christ.

71

In short, what we have in the New Testament is basically two distinct prophetic streams functioning in two different contexts, the one being prophetic ministry in the emerging congregations of apostolic Christianity, the other being the prophetic ministry of Jesus himself. This is not the same divide which we find in the Old Testament as described by Brueggemann, where the two types of prophecy are almost mutually exclusive. In the New Testament they may appear to be so, but in fact they come together as complementary components in the ministry of the church.

On the one hand, there are those charismatic prophets who speak a word of the Lord to congregations which are increasingly separate from Judaism and perceive themselves as existing in an hostile environment awaiting the Parousia. As in the Letters to the Seven Churches, these churches live in dependence on the word of the Lord who is alive in their midst through the Spirit. On the other hand, there is Jesus who not only identifies himself with the Hebrew prophets, but also fulfils their mission to Israel and the world, and who like the prophets is put to death by those in religious and political authority.[20] Yet, as we have already noted, the New Testament gospels which proclaim Jesus and the kingdom of God are also addressed to congregations in specific social contexts. The question is how are these two New Testament prophetic streams to be related to each other and expressed in the life of the church today? There is a prior question. What happened to the prophetic tradition in the development of the church so that prophecy of either stream became the exception rather than the rule, peripheral to the life of the church rather than part of its very foundation? A look at the way in which prophecy died in traditional Christianity may help us understand how it is still quenched today, and also how the spirit of prophecy may be revived.

The Domestication and Rediscovery of Prophecy

In the course of Christian history both streams, that of charismatic prophets concerned about the faithfulness of the church to the Jesus tradition in the present day and therefore concerned about the ongoing renewal of the church, and social prophets seeking to proclaim the message of Jesus and the kingdom of God in the world, have been suppressed in the interests of church and political authority and unity. Prophets still have an honoured place in the second century *Didache*, but already in Ignatius the role of the prophet is being annexed by the centralisation of ministries in the episcopate.[21] To quote Aune with regard to the charismatic, congregational prophets: 'With the institutionalisation of its authority structures, prophecy became redundant as well as dysfunctional.' Their role 'as articulators of the norms, values, and decisions of the invisible head of the church was taken over by the visible figures of the teacher, the preacher, theologian and church leader.'[22] Whereas in the *Didache* prophets even preside at the eucharist, this task along with that of prophecy soon becomes the prerogative of the bishop. It is a casualty of the process to which we referred earlier, whereby the charismata of the many become the privilege of the few.

This development was disastrous for the ministry of the church. But it was also understandable, given our knowledge of the way in which institutions grow, and, more specifically in view of the long delayed Parousia and the schismatic threat which prophetic movements such as Montanism posed for the church. But the institutionalised over-reaction 'quenched the Spirit' to such an extent that prophecy along with some other charismatic gifts of ministry became sectarian or were pushed onto the periphery of the life of the church. Prophetic ministry was virtu-

73

ally excluded from the task of leadership in the church and, on the contrary, was regarded as detrimental to it. But the process also reflects the acculturation of the church whereby the community of faith began to pattern itself according to the prevailing social status quo. As a result not only prophecy but the egalitarian character of the early Christian communities was gradually surrendered, and cultural norms relating, for example, to slaves and women were adopted.

In a way similar to the domestication of the charismatic prophets in the primitive church, and often in tandem, the eschatological radicality of Jesus' own mission as prophetic Messiah was suppressed in the development of Christology and Trinitarian theology. This was not always intentional, but radical discipleship and social criticism were pushed to the peripheries of the church. They survived in the rise of monasticism and religious orders, and in sectarian movements which invariably suffered greatly at the hands of both church and secular authorities. This shift away from radical discipleship was partly the result of the re-thinking of eschatology in view of the delayed Parousia, and the growing tendency to identify the church, especially the church triumphant, and later even the Holy Roman Empire, with the kingdom of God. It does not mean that the development of Trinitarian theology was misguided or unbiblical, but rather that its separation from its historical base in Jesus and the kingdom of God had results contrary to its intention, and led to its political and ecclesiastical misuse.[23]

Once Christology, or theology generally, is sundered from Jesus' proclamation and embodiment of the reign of God in the world, it loses its critical, prophetic character and can be misused to serve the interests of the state and a triumphalist church. Once the prophetic office of Christ becomes simply part of a dogmatic system and no longer

74

expresses the ministry of Jesus as fulfiller of the prophetic tradition as social and cultic critique, then it undermines that office. As Calvin himself said of the 'papists' of his day in this very connection, 'they are satisfied with the vain pretence of the name, and strip him of his power and dignity.'[24] Calvin however, even in affirming Jesus' prophetic office, failed to grasp its critical implications for society despite the fact that his theology had a socio-political dimension and exalted Jesus as king over all reality.[25]

Thus in the process of the institutionalisation of the church and its Constantinian establishment, as well as in the development of the Holy Roman Empire, the charismatic prophet and the prophet Messiah were both domesticated. This has been a recurring pattern in Christian history following periods of renewal or reform, and it remains so today. Prophetic, charismatic leadership and ministry, by their very nature, pose a problem for the institutional church and its leaders. Must this inevitably be so? And must prophets necessarily be, as Max Weber indicates, persons who, by definition, are in tension or conflict with priest and pastor, and often lonely and peripheral figures?[26] Must prophets always remain in an uneasy relationship to both church leadership and the church itself, sometimes being encouraged but often functioning without honour and not seldom being crucified? To go further, is it possible to reinstate the ministry of prophecy alongside that of other ministries within the life of the mainline churches? Or, as an alternative, is it possible for the ordained leadership of the church to be engaged in prophetic ministry? Finally, is it possible for the church itself to be prophetic and, at the same time, maintain its unity and fulfil its pastoral task?

Whatever the answers to these questions, the church today, in its mission to the world and in its own pastoral practice, has to discover how vital prophecy is to its own life and its social praxis. And therefore, however the prophetic ministry is structured, it is essential that the church and its leaders understand the necessity of prophecy and their own responsibility towards prophetic ministry in the life of the church. The word of prophecy is always addressed first of all to the community of faith. That is where the judgment of God begins because without this the church cannot fulfil its responsibility within the world. The church can only be the church insofar as it is self-critical in the light of the word of the Lord. For this reason it needs the prophetic insight, discernment and challenge of its prophets. 'What becomes of a Church in which the *prophets* are silent?' asks Hans Kung.

> What becomes of a Church in which there is no one who gives direct expression in words to the promptings of the Spirit, even if in a different form from the prophets of Paul's time; a Church in which there is no one with a conviction of his calling and responsibility to illuminate the Church's path in both present and future in a particular situation? A Church in which the prophets have to keep silent declines, and becomes a spiritless organisation.[27]

Sometimes, fortunately for the church, when its own prophets are silenced, the world raises others who in anger, cynicism or alienated longing for the church to be true to itself, force the church to self-examination. In the South African context, as elsewhere, this has often been done by poets, novelists and dramatists, some who believe, but most who do not. So too, the great critics of religion, Ludwig Feuerbach, Karl Marx or Sigmund Freud, however much we may disagree with their premises, function as iconoclasts, challenging the church to examine its life and witness. Writing as a Marxist who nevertheless takes Jesus and his message very seriously, Milan Machovec in *A Marxist Looks at Jesus* put it very simply and candidly:

76

If we study carefully the history of those who opposed Christianity as the worship of a divinised Jesus, we discover the very interesting and obviously characteristic fact that these polemicists and critics hardly ever blamed Christians for being disciples of Jesus, but rather reproached them with *not* being truly his disciples, with betraying his cause.[28]

Increasingly it is being realised today, however, that the most significant critics of the church are not the intellectual giants such as we have mentioned, but the poor and oppressed peoples. Their critique may be premised on the rejection of faith in God but it is the result of oppressive suffering rather than academic argument. This challenge will confront us again in the next chapter. But there are others who are poor and oppressed, not least in South Africa, who do believe, who are, in fact, the majority in the Christian church, and whose presence constitutes a radical prophetic challenge to the church. It forces the church, if the church has eyes to see, to perceive how things look 'from below', from the perspective of those who suffer. Whereas the church may be able to counter the challenges of its intellectual critics through the skills of its own academic and professional theologians, it can only respond to the challenge of the poor and oppressed in its midst by listening to their cries and responding in solidarity with their struggle for justice. This, more than anything else, requires that the church read Scripture with new eyes.

In a lecture given at the University of Cape Town in 1986, the South African Dominican theologian, Albert Nolan, author of the best-seller, *Jesus before Christianity*, addressed the subject of academic freedom in a way which speaks directly to our theme. Referring to the fact that 'oppression is a fundamental category of Biblical theology', he pointed out that 'until recently every Christian scholar or theologian had consistently overlooked it. They had simply never noticed at all that oppression was a theme in the Bible.' While this is not strictly true, as heirs of the Radical Reformation would point out, it is true enough. But Nolan went on to ask the pertinent question: 'With the tremendous amount of scholarship, learning and dedication that has been put into the study of the Bible over the centuries, how is it possible that everyone missed what is now regarded as a fundamental category of the Biblical message.' His answer? 'The fact that we did not belong to the oppressed classes of people in the world or have any sympathetic contact with oppressed people made us totally blind to what the Bible was saying so insistently and so graphically about oppression.' The change came about, Nolan argues, when theologians in Latin America encouraged the poor and oppressed to read the Bible in terms of their existential plight. Then something else happened. The people not only helped the scholars to see something they had missed, but the scholars began to exercise their talents in new ways which served the interests of those who suffered and not simply the interests of scholarship, the political status quo, or the institutional church. It was not that the academic theological task became redundant, but it took on new life, a new urgency and a new focus. The prophetic critique of the poor had set them free to be true to their vocation.[29] This is a powerful illustration of the relationship between the task of academic theology and that of the pastor or priest within the community of faith.

Writing ten years ago, the British theologian Daniel Jenkins contended that

the chief reason why British churches are weak today is that they do not believe enough in the Christian God whom they profess to serve. This is why they lack the vitality and the independence of judgement to stand back from their own situation and see themselves and their relation to the

78

society of which they are part in the right perspective and
then to speak with prophetic authority.[30]

Perspective is fundamental to prophecy, and it is the
responsibility of the practical theologian in doing critical,
prophetic theology, to question his or her perspectives,
those of the community of faith and the church in general,
in terms of whose interests prophecy is serving. Thus
we are back at Brueggemann's fundamental distinction
between court prophets and liberation prophets; those
serving their own interests and that of their race or class, or
those serving the interests of God's transformation of the
world.

A church which is open to the prophetic word of the Lord
is a church which is willing to allow itself to be caught up
through the Spirit into the Messianic ministry of the crucified Lord to the world. It is thus a confessing church
engaged in a critical, liberating task in the world. The prophetic task in the life of the congregation, and the prophetic
ministry to society, are in the end, however structured, the
ministry of Jesus through the same Spirit speaking both to
the church and to the world. The tradition of the prophet
Messiah who is Lord becomes concrete in each new historical context. But the prophetic word and deed do not arise
out of the context; their roots are deeper in the tradition of
faith, hope and love embodied in worship and praise, the
proclamation of the Word of God and eucharistic fellowship. It was while he 'was in the Spirit on the Lord's day'
that John heard the prophetic word for the Seven
Churches; so it is today.

It is within many communities of faith the world over that
the prophetic word arises, within the context of praise, as
the community of faith listens, prays, and fellowships
together in the breaking of bread. Once again we are affirming with the Scriptures of both Testaments, as well as with

Bengt Sundkler and the churches in Africa, the charismatic character of prophetic ministry. That is, the quality of charism, of a gift which is given, a vision which comes from beyond even in the midst of the struggle. In the words of Daniel Hardy and David Ford after reflecting on prophecy in the Old Testament:

> The prophets were charismatic men and women who had the gift of intimacy with Yahweh. Prophecy grew from the liturgy, interpreting its message and relating it to the present situation . . . The prophet is typically one who is so taken up into worship and the vision that is given by God in it that he acts as a spokesman for God to the people and for the people to God.[31]

In our final chapter we shall examine the way in which this prophetic ministry is integrally related to the worship and praise of the church. But one last word from Hardy and Ford brings together several of the themes we have been exploring thus far in relating theology, pastoral concern and prophecy to each other:

> To praise and know God is itself prophetic. It affirms the most comprehensive truth of history and the future. It is an act of discernment and committed response that lets God be God, and so both criticises and encourages in each situation. 'God is' is the supreme prophetic statement, the discernment which can illuminate all discernment and action. But it is not a statement about something static and fixed: it is about a God who is alive, active, listening and communicating. To recognise this God in each situation is always the most urgent priority.[32]

The first chapter of the Report of the Review Group on Ministerial Training in the United Reformed Church in England, *Preparing Today for Tomorrow's Ministry*, published in 1982, begins: 'Jesus came announcing the kingdom of

God.'[33] Further on, the Report applies this to the ordained ministry in a way which relates directly to what we have been saying:

> Our thinking about ministry in this kind of society must begin from the fact that the Gospel is about the coming of God's reign over all people and all things. The Gospel is good news of that coming reign. The ministry of this Gospel would be misdirected if its central concern was with the 'success' of the Church. Its concern is that the Church may be a credible sign and foretaste of the Kingdom – of that kingly rule which is exercised from the cross.[34]

Prophecy, Social Analysis and Praxis

The question is: how is prophetic ministry to be embodied in the life of the church and especially the local congregation? We shall start by considering the question as to whether or not the church itself should be a prophetic community. Let us begin by examining the two basic options. Firstly, it can be argued, as does Robin Gill in *Prophecy and Praxis*, that the church itself cannot be prophetic, but it needs prophets and it must enable them to fulfil their task as social and ecclesial critics. Gill's rationale for this is the fact that prophecy by its very nature must be partisan in its interpretation of the gospel and society, and therefore divisive and sectarian.[35] 'My own suggestion,' Gill writes, 'is that churches as *churches* largely abandon Christian prophecy and rely instead upon the individual prophets in their midst.'[36] This, for Gill, is not a downgrading of prophecy, but rather an enabling of prophecy without the church surrendering its necessary pastoral or priestly, and invariably ambiguous, relationship to society.

81

Secondly, contrary to Gill's thesis, is the position represented by the contributions in Ambler and Haslam's *Agenda for Prophets*. As Ambler himself writes: 'Christianity can and should be embodied in a prophetic community, accepting its minority role but relating its specific religious practice to a wider secular practice for the transformation of society.'[37] It is only in this way that the church can exercise its pastoral responsibility to society. A similar position is adopted in North America by the essayists in *The Pastor as Prophet*.[38]

The comparison between Gill's position and that of the authors of *Agenda for Prophets* is partly the result of two different ecclesiastical traditions in England, the one more establishment in ethos and the other non-conformist. But it is even more the case that the variations result from two different analyses of society. This becomes clear on those occasions when Gill makes reference to the prophetic task of the church in South Africa where the issues are far clearer and less ambiguous than in contemporary Britain. In such abnormal situations, Gill recognises, the church itself will have to become prophetic and try to be priestly on that basis, difficult as it may be. 'Certain regimes' writes Gill, 'are so evidently opposed to the Gospel that churches can take and in fact have taken, a prophetic stand against.'[39] But that, Gill maintains, is not the case in Britain. Although Peter Hinchliff in *Holiness and Politics* takes a similar line, he nevertheless qualifies Gill's position by speaking, in the tradition of William Temple, of the church as the critic of society and the individual Christian as the active social reformer.[40]

Within the South African churches there is much debate on the proper role of the church within the social arena. Allowing for some variation in style and emphasis, it is nevertheless possible to say that all those churches which have opposed apartheid through the years have adopted a prophetic stance *as churches.* It may also be said, at least in theory, that the white Dutch Reformed church in its official documents and in continuity with its Reformed heritage, claims the right of the church to speak prophetically to the nation. At the same time, the Dutch Reformed Church has assumed an established church mentality which not only results in silence when it should speak but also in the silencing of individual prophets within its boundaries. Nevertheless, the real differences between the churches is not at the level of church-state theory. It arises out of different social perceptions and analysis, a different reading of Scripture, and different group interests and commitments. Thus while all churches may agree on the need for justice in society, they disagree on what justice entails in politically concrete terms.

But even then we must go further and note the protest of *The Kairos Document* which questions the prophetic integrity of those churches which have, in principle, opposed apartheid. This is not an altogether fair accusation, but neither is it without foundation. Over against 'church theology', and in the name of 'prophetic theology', the Kairos theologians call for a more rigorous social analysis and committed praxis. Thus the conflict between the prophetic statements of churches in South Africa regarding the social situation is a vivid illustration that the spirit and word of prophecy needs to be tested. The church can be prophetic in the liberatory tradition of social criticism; it can also be prophetic in the tradition of the court prophets who cry 'Peace, peace, when there is no peace.'

In the same way, the essayists in *Agenda for Prophets* have a different perception and analysis of British society to that of the more establishment position adopted by Gill, and therefore a different prescription for Christian praxis.

Stephen Yeo, for example, discerns within British society the first phases of an emergent fascism. 'Which is why' he writes, 'alternative prophecy is so urgent now.' This prophetic task means, Yeo continues,

> naming and analysing the contradictions (i.e. in British society) in the light of our understanding of what it is to be human in society in the light of God's purposes, and daring to advocate the resolution of the contradictions on the side of righteousness, not at a millenial 'revolutionary' stroke but through a deliberately chosen process of struggle which, because we are Christians, prefigures the ends in the means.[41]

In comparison with *Prophecy and Praxis*, the social analysis which undergirds the essays in *Agenda for Prophets* is radical and sometimes Marxian in orientation rather than reformist; its social portrait is thus more critical of British society; its vision for the church and its task is more radically prophetic; it is committed to a liberation style of doing theology, and therefore to an understanding of theology as critical reflection on the present praxis of the church. There is, in fact, in *Agenda for Prophets* a greater sense of being engaged in a dynamic historical project to transform British society than is apparent in *Prophecy and Praxis*. Thus Ambler sees the church as critically engaged in the secular project of social and cultural transformation but from within its prophetic, liberatory tradition.

> In particular it can serve that project by making its practice prophetic, rehearsing the tradition of prophecy in a struggle for, and witness to, the promised peace and justice, maintaining its characteristic stance in relation to the present situation. It can give a depth of meaning to the historical project which it would not otherwise have, whilst in the same process it can establish its own meaning in a particular historical situation.[42]

84

This sense of the church participating in an historical project relates directly to our earlier comments on the task of the church as participation in the *missio Dei*, and we will pick up the theme again in the final chapter when we reflect on the theological formation of the People of God.

The most penetrating review of *Agenda for Prophets* was that of Ronald Preston,[43] who develops his position more fully in *Church and Society in the Late Twentieth Century*. His position is dialectically juxtaposed between that of Gill and *Agenda for the Prophets*, rejecting as he does the need for affirming either of the polarities as exclusive.

> Profound conviction at the centre and an indefinite boundary at the periphery might be thought a sociological monstrosity, combining the features of a sect and church. But it is not impossible. Indeed, it is a truly catholic position.[44]

Clearly, Preston sees the need for an ongoing social analysis which in turn should determine the prophetic character and response of the church, rather than the adoption of a static position which only allows for rare exceptions. But Preston's main concern regarding the approach taken by *Agenda for Prophets* is his fear that particular positions will be absolutised as 'the will of God' for us. Thus he provides us with a salutary reminder of the danger of the prophetic approach:

> The Old Testament prophets provide dangerous models of black and white denunciations which can hinder Christians from perceiving the ambiguities and ambivalences involved in moral discernment in relation to detailed situations and policies. The inevitable uncertainties at this level mean that the changing details must not be identified too simply with God's Word.[45]

We certainly need to acknowledge the danger to which Preston points, and the need to be constantly aware of equating one's own perceptions with the prophetic 'Thus says the Lord'. Triumphalist 'prophecy' which arises out of self-righteousness, or false prophecy which arises out of self-interest, is clearly not in continuity with the prophetic tradition of which we speak. But quite apart from these obvious examples of the misuse of its authority, it has not been unknown for the church to speak with prophetic authority on issues about which it had little knowledge, and thereby to lend its support to doubtful causes. Nevertheless, it would be a sad, even fatal day for the church if it could never come down off the fence and say, as Dietrich Bonhoeffer did: 'this is God's Word to us here and now.'

> The church must be able to say the Word of God, the word of authority, here and now, in the most concrete way possible, from knowledge of the situation. The church may not therefore preach timeless principles, however true, but only commandments which are true today. God is 'always' *God* to us *'today'*.[46]

The alternative is the church, as Barth put it, making 'a habit of coming to the scene too late, of entering the fray only when its opinions no longer involve any risk and can no longer exert any particular influence'.[47]

Once again we are back at the indispensable role to be played by the practical theologian, and, as we shall see, the theological insight and discernment of the People as a whole. Before the prophetic word can be uttered with any authority, the community of faith and its prophets need to exercise self-criticism (critical reflection on praxis), engage in careful analysis of the situation which needs to be addressed, and discern what the Biblical message is which needs to be proclaimed here and now. This requires the ongoing theological formation of the People of God so that through the preaching of the Word, pastoral care and liturgical celebration, a prophetically discerning community takes root and exercises its ministry in each place.

In order to make this process more specific and concrete, and in anticipation of our discussion on the theological formation of the People of God, I wish to inject at this point what Joe Holland and Peter Henriot have called the 'pastoral circle'.[48] This is one significant way whereby the prophetic word and deed can become integral to the life of the church and its pastoral practice. It provides a methodological answer to the question with which we began this section: how is prophetic ministry to be embodied in the life of the church and especially the local congregation?

Holland and Henriot refer to four moments in the pastoral-hermeneutic circle.[49] The first they call the moment of *insertion*.

> This locates the geography of our pastoral responses in the lived experience of individuals and communities. What people are feeling, what they are undergoing, how they are responding – these are the experiences that constitute primary data.

There are many moments of insertion within the average congregation, not only moments when pastoral care is most needed because of human pain or bereavement, but also when the community of faith is struggling to be faithful to its prophetic task. In the South African context such moments have become quite critical. By way of illustration, the point of insertion for a black pastor in a South African township may well be, as it has been for many, the funeral of a church member shot dead by the police. Related to this is the problem of violence which confronts many a pastor and congregation where, for example, young blacks may feel that there is no hope except through the barrel of a gun. Another critical issue is that of suffering, a 'moment of insertion' which every pastor encounters day by day, but which takes on a new dimension when it is related to oppression. In the next chapter we will focus on this issue as one which requires urgent theological reflection in our situation.

The second moment to which Holland and Henriot refer, which is the beginning of an attempt to understand these experiences, is that of *social analysis*. This is also of fundamental importance for the Kairos theologians: 'the first task of a prophetic theology for our times would be an attempt at social analysis or what Jesus would call "reading the signs of the times" (Mt. 16:3) or "interpreting this KAIROS" (Lk. 12:56).' But *The Kairos Document* does not say precisely what this implies. Holland and Henriot spell it out in the following way:

> Social analysis examines causes, probes consequences, delineates linkages, and identifies actors. It helps make sense of experiences by putting them into a broader picture and drawing the connections between them.

Or,

> Social analysis can be defined as the effort to obtain a more complete picture of a social situation by exploring its *historical and structural relationships.* Social analysis serves as a tool that permits us to grasp the reality with which we are dealing.[50]

While 'social analysis' may sound like a very sophisticated operation and, indeed, it can and often must be so, Holland and Henriot emphasise that it is not beyond the ability of any community which seriously seeks to understand what is happening within the society of which it is a part. Indeed, they write: 'social analysis is simply an extension of the principle of discernment, moving from the personal realm to the social.'[51]

This leads to the third moment, *theological reflection*, which is

> an effort to understand more broadly and deeply the ana-
> lysed experience in the light of living faith, scripture,
> church social teaching, and the resources of tradition. The
> Word of God brought to bear upon the situation raises new
> questions, suggests new insights, and opens new responses.

In the final chapter we shall deal more fully with the interaction of critical theological reflection and the communication of the Word in the preaching, teaching, pastoral care
and liturgical life of the Christian community. But such
communication has to be wedded to the mission-praxis of
the community in the world.

Thus we come to the final moment in Holland and Henriot's pastoral-hermeneutic circle. This is the crucial stage
of *pastoral planning* in which the community decides on what
they now discern to be God's will for them, what it is they
are now called to be as the People of God and what action
this requires in the world. *It is precisely at this point that the
pastor as practical theologian becomes an enabler of prophetic words
and deeds within the congregation.* And so the circle, or spiral
continues, because such action leads to further analysis,
critical theological reflection and planning. In this way the
witness or action of the church or the Christian becomes,
strictly speaking, praxis.

Praxis, while literally meaning practice, has in critical
theory come to mean practice or action which is subject to
critical reflection. That is, action which is not blind or
undirected, but action shaped by a particular theory, set of
values and goals.[52] In the moment of *critical reflection* theology functions as critical theory. Only in this way can praxis really communicate the Word of God, and only through
such pastoral practice is the Word of God communicated.

It is in this sense that we may understand Bonhoeffer's contention that 'the *first* confession of the Christian community before the world is the *deed* which interprets itself.'[53]

Prophets and Pastors: An African Perspective

The debate about the relationship between priests and prophets in religious communities has been central to the sociology of religion. Almost invariably, as we have already noted, their respective roles have been regarded as in competition with each other so that the charismatic authority of the prophet is perceived as a threat to the institutional authority of the priest and vice versa. 'The moral outrage that fuels the fires of prophetic calling' seems, as Stanley Hauerwas puts it, 'incompatible with the kind of openness necessary to being a caring pastor.'[54] We have, nevertheless, argued the need for the church to be prophetic, and the need in the life of the church for prophets who keep the church in mind of the radical demands of the reign of God in Jesus Christ in the world. This implies that the relationship between pastor or priest and prophet is crucial, and that it is entirely unsatisfactory for them to be in a state of competition or mutual rejection.

In the final chapter we shall return to this theme when we consider the important role which the ordained minister as pastor has to fulfil in enabling the community of faith to become a prophetic community. But in conclusion to this chapter we shall seek to learn a little from a segment of the church in Africa where pastors and prophets coexist in a way that is salutary for what we are considering. I refer to those African indigenous churches, particularly those which scholars label Zionist (this has nothing to do with

Jewish Zionism, nor is it to be equated with the very large, black but socially conservative Zionist Christian Church in South Africa), where the charismatic prophet and the institutionalised bishop or pastor share together as leaders within the congregation. Our focus in reflecting on this pattern of collegiality is the relationship between pastor and prophet rather than the content of their respective ministries.

In an illuminating passage in his article 'Prophet and Preacher: An Essential Partnership in the Work of Zion', J.P. Kiernan writes:

> Despite the appearances of being at cross purposes, prophet and preacher form the essential partnership which is the core of Zionist social organisation. It is precisely because they act differently upon the band, the one consolidating and the other fragmenting it, that their roles neatly complement one another. That this is so becomes clear by considering the outcome of prophetic intervention. A prophet is successful to the extent that his verdicts are accepted, but he does not gain his acceptance unless and until the treatment he advocates is put into action. At this point, the cooperation of the minister becomes crucial; he it is who must bless and transfer items either for medicinal consumption or for protective wearing. Timing this part of the treatment is entirely in his hands and undue delay can damage a prophet's reputation. Nevertheless, the minister needs the prophetic direction before he can proceed to treatment just as much as the prophet requires the minister's ratification. Prophet and preacher share in a common enterprise, that of constantly restructuring the band. They are partners in this reconstruction and the division of labour between them is closely observed.[55]

Kiernan goes on to show that Zionist congregations condemn what he calls 'pirate prophets', those who function without commitment to the community and therefore without relating positively to its leadership and the preaching of Scripture. 'Without this institutional setting' writes Kiernan, 'a prophet in Zionist eyes is no better than an *isangoma* (diviner) or *inyanga* (herbalist) whose activities are regarded as commercial, anarchic and malevolent.'[56]

There are, of course, some major differences between an African indigenous church congregation and those of white, middle-class people whether in South Africa or elsewhere. For one thing, the Zionist congregations do not have to worry a great deal about the maintenance of property, the payment of clergy salaries, or the demands of denominational authorities. Indeed, it is often precisely these material factors which mitigate against genuine prophecy. Moreover, the indigenous congregations which Kiernan describes are small, closely knit groups of people whose life together meets a very real felt need – communal support and healing in the face of shared poverty, discrimination and social disintegration. The leadership of the communities is not a highly trained elite who, by virtue of their education and theological training have been set apart from the community, but often members of the particular group to which they have been called to minister. The leadership of the Zionist communities arises from within and learns its skills and discovers its gifts in the community. Furthermore, and this is obviously of crucial importance for our comparison, the charismatic prophet is, above all else, the healer rather than the social critic. The question as to whether these are mutually exclusive, simply unrelated or organically inseparable is one which we will explore later and answer in terms of the third option.

It is not possible to generalise about the role of the prophet in such a context and the role of the prophet in a community of social and economic privilege. In the latter, the prophet might need to be, as Amos was, an outsider, almost a pirate prophet! And yet, there are important insights in the relationship between the prophets and bishops of Zion which we would do well to ponder. In doing so we might keep in mind the similarities between what Kiernan describes and the 'base communities' of Latin America. We would also do well not to romanticise them.

First of all, the prophet and the pastor are normally two distinct people, as is usually also the pattern in the Pauline congregations in the New Testament. This does not mean that their offices cannot be conflated, but it does indicate that the two tasks are difficult to hold together in one person. The norm should probably be two distinct offices, even though there may be those ministers who are able to be prophets while they remain pastors. The personality factor, for both prophets and pastors, must be kept in mind, because we are not talking primarily about offices, but about people and charisms. There are some people who are more able to combine these tasks than others simply by virtue of their personality, gifts and skills at communication – though this should not be regarded as an excuse any more than it was for those Old Testament prophets who tried to escape the imperative of God.

Secondly, as in the New Testament the functioning of both prophet and pastor in the indigenous or Zionist congregation requires community support and acceptance, even though their authority as such is hierarchical and derives, as it were, from the Lord. From this we may say that one of the essential tasks of leadership within the church is to nurture and support those who have the gift of genuine prophecy and, at the same time, to equip and enable the church to be responsive to the Word of the Lord which they may utter. It may well be that some of the prophets which the community of faith needs to hear most are beyond the walls, indeed, people who have in anger rejected it in the name of justice and righteousness. Hence Brueggemann's description of the task of prophetic ministry is apt: 'to nurture, nourish, and evoke a consciousness and perception alternative to the consciousness and perception of the dominant culture around us.'[57] The theological task of the pastor, whether he or she also functions as prophet, is that of discernment between true and false prophecy, so that the congregation may respond to the genuine prophetic word as faithfully as possible in their context. This gift of discernment is not the exclusive possession of the pastor; it is a gift given to the community and is exercised by the community. But, once again, it is the pastor's responsibility to see that it is exercised. In the same way, not every pastor will be, or can be, a prophet; but every pastor should be an enabler of prophecy.

Thirdly, the role of prophet and pastor are regarded as complementary. This does not mean there is no tension between them, but that the one cannot properly function without the other. As Martin West has shown, the tensions often become so acute that congregations are split. This is one reason for the proliferation of indigenous churches, and one reason why in the early Christian church charismatic leadership was eventually suppressed. An alternate model, and West has also pointed this out, is that prophet and pastor are either embodied in a wife and husband team, with the wife being the prophet, or else conflated in the office of one person.[58]

In most congregations with which many of us are familiar, the pastor often has to be the prophet as well. But whether or not the prophet is the pastor or someone else, what is essential is that the prophetic ministry be exercised, and that it be exercised pastorally. Commenting on Reinhold Niebuhr's sermons, his biographer Richard Fox writes that they consistently combined priestly and prophetic postures: a priestly gospel of hope for coping with everyday perplexities and tragedies of everyday life; a prophetic gospel of repentance for confronting personal sin and social evil.[59]

Just as justice and love are always in tension, but always necessary to each other, so the community of faith needs pastors and prophets in order to become a community of caring people, people who care enough about others that they are also willing to become a community of prophets who seek to transcend their own cultural and social captivities and seek to obey the Word of God today.

Towards the end of his very helpful study of prophetic ministry entitled *Prophetic Imagination*, Walter Brueggemann reflects something of the inner tension within every pastor in the struggle to be a faithful prophet within the congregation. His words are an appropriate conclusion, and they also refer us back again to the fact that the ordained ministry is a very human affair made possible only by the grace of God, the charism of the Spirit. Brueggemann writes:

> as I reflect on ministry, and especially my ministry, I know in the hidden places that the real restraints are not in my understanding or in the receptivity of other people. Rather, the restraints come from my own unsureness about this perception. I discover that I am as bourgeois and obdurate as any to whom I might minister. I, like most of the others, am unsure that the royal road is not the best and the royal community the one which governs the real 'goodies'. I, like most of the others, am unsure that the alternative community inclusive of the poor, hungry, and grieving is really the wave of God's future. We are indeed 'like people, like priest' (Hosea 4:9). That very likely is the situation among many of us in ministry and there is no unanguished way out of it. It does make clear to us that our ministry will always be practised through our own conflicted selves.[60]

CHAPTER THREE

Oppressive Suffering, Theological Reflection, and Christian Solidarity

Within a few weeks of my being ordained to the ministry and inducted to serve in a congregation in Durban, a young boy belonging to our Sunday School was knocked down and killed by a drunken driver. If I recall correctly, his funeral was the first I had ever conducted. Certainly my stumbling attempt to minister to his parents, initially in silent solidarity, but then in trying to help them make sense out of something beyond comprehension, was my 'moment of insertion' in the task of ministry. Such experiences are almost part of the weekly routine of many ministers in large and busy parishes, but each occasion is a challenge to faith. Words sound hollow, and the traditional arguments which try to reconcile belief in a loving and almighty God with human suffering seem so trite. How much more is this the case when the cause of the suffering is political and social oppression. If ever a pastor is forced to be a practical theologian it is at such moments, for what can it possibly mean to 'know God' when God seems totally absent and unconcerned about our anguish and pain? Here the analysis of experience, theological reflection, and pastoral practice all come together in an inseparable way and, indeed, theology finally becomes prayer.

An Excess of Suffering

Few contemporary theologians have wrestled with the problem of human suffering with such historical grasp and theological insight as Edward Schillebeeckx. Towards the end of his monumental study *Christ: the Experience of Jesus as Lord,* Schillebeeckx acknowledges some positive features about suffering. There 'are certain forms of suffering which enrich our humanity'; 'a certain dose of suffering undergone can make us sensitive' to others; 'a certain amount of suffering transforms' us and others. But he continues:

> Despite all these true considerations ... there is an *excess* of suffering and evil in our history. There is a barbarous excess, for all the explanations and interpretations. There is too much *unmerited* and *senseless* suffering for us to be able to give an ethical, hermeneutical and ontological analysis of our disaster. There is suffering which is not even suffering 'for a good cause', but suffering in which men, without finding meaning for themselves, are simply made the crude victims of an evil cause which serves others. Furthermore, this suffering is the alpha and omega of the whole history of mankind; it is the scarlet thread by which this historical fragment is recognisable as human history: history is 'ar ecumene of suffering'.[1]

In the light of this excess suffering which surrounds us, directly affecting men, women and children as a fact of daily personal experience, it seems almost obscene to discuss it in an academic manner. In relation to the tragic pain and anguish which has been experienced in South Africa during these past few years, and for many years previously by black people in particular, it is also a serious question whether a white theologian like myself can make any contribution to the subject.

It is true, of course, that none of us is exempt from suffering of some kind, for suffering is built into the fabric of human existence. Moreover, who knows what experience of suffering, pain and anguish awaits us around the corner of our lives. There are varieties of suffering, and different degrees to which people have to suffer. Yet, for many of us the privilege of class and race have enabled us thus far to escape the excess of senseless and unmerited suffering to which Schillebeeckx refers. We may be exposed to and moved by the horrors of starvation as we watch news bulletins on Ethiopia flash across our television screens. But we personally know little about hunger. We may be angered and pained by events in our own country which have dehumanised people and destroyed communities, events seldom confronting us on TV, yet few of us know what it means to be uprooted from our homes and dumped elsewhere.

At the outset, then, it should be clear that my focus here is not upon the general problem of suffering, but upon the problem of the excessive suffering of people, and particularly upon what might be called oppressive suffering, that is, suffering as a result of the inhumanity and violence of others. This does not imply that suffering in more general terms is no longer a theological problem, but an immense amount has already been said and written about it. Moreover, as Johann Baptist Metz has reminded us, speaking about 'suffering in general' is dangerous in the sense that it not only results in vagueness but by reducing all suffering to the same level ('Does a rich playboy in his luxury bungalow not suffer?' 'Do not whites in South Africa also suffer?') it prevents us from really facing the challenge of oppressive suffering.[2]

Much, it is true, has also been written and said about oppressive suffering, and there is also the danger here that we may relapse into vague generalities and so avoid its challenge. Yet it is my intention to focus upon oppressive suffering as a theological problem specifically within the South African context, and this I suspect has not been done very often.[3] Thus, just as the contemporary theological debate on suffering has been sparked off by events such as the Holocaust and Hiroshima, so within our own context, theological reflection on suffering is called for by the reality of apartheid, and should be grounded in it. Whether we who are white South Africans like it or not, whether we regard it as fair or not, in the annals of history, apartheid will be bracketed with the Holocaust and similar events as twentieth century examples of excessive, unmerited and oppressive suffering.

Reflections such as these have made me rather ambivalent about writing on the subject. Would we not learn more if we listened to black colleagues who have suffered greatly through the inhumanity of apartheid, or if we opened our ears to the cries of agony which arise from the townships. We know when we hear the authentic voice of suffering because it moves us to silence. 'A man', writes Schillebeeckx, 'who has become mature through suffering compels wonderment, deep admiration, and reduces one to silence; one finds oneself enriched by the experience of such gentle wisdom which has grown through life.'[4] What possible contribution can a white, middle-class theologian make to our understanding of suffering, then, if he has no direct experience of its awful reality?

Forgive these personal reflections, but nothing has perplexed me more in pondering upon this theme. And yet, because this is so, and because it may well be so for many others, perhaps it is the place to begin. Unlike Job's comforters we dare not rush in with easy answers drafted in our studies, answers which may reflect reasonable theory but little wisdom, answers which prevent us from moving beyond an academic problem to Christian solidarity with those who suffer.

At a time of immense suffering in her homeland in 1940, the Russian emigre Iulia de Beausobre gave a remarkable series of lectures in England entitled *Creative Suffering*. 'I feel convinced' she said, 'that when we strive to eliminate bodily, economic and environmental suffering we are dealing (rightly indeed and often wisely) with nothing more than a flagrant symptom, a surface occurrence. The root of the question lies much deeper ...' It is ultimately a theological issue. Yet, she continued,

> the enigma of suffering cannot be the concern of theologians alone. Indeed, though the theologian usually comes to such matters after much time spent in acquiring extensive but inevitably second-hand knowledge, of great but less obviously universal interest, yet suffering seems quite lately to have acquired a sweep, a vigour, a variety and a precision that it lacked in former times, so that most people are today aware of an astonishing extent of suffering going on all around them. .... And since knowledge is always, even with the least imaginative of us, a kind of participation, we can all be said to take part, if only dimly and at second hand, in a great deal of suffering. But there are countries, and Russia is one of them, where first-hand knowledge of suffering has become universal, where every man, woman and not infrequently many a child, is directly confronted with the thing itself, with suffering as a fact of personal experience.[5]

While Iulia de Beausobre assumes that all theologians are by the very nature of their vocation academically aloof, an assumption that must not go unchallenged, many who are academic theologians may well reflect on suffering 'only dimly and at second-hand'. Yet as human beings who live in a world of pain, as South Africans who are part of a society in travail and grief, as pastors caring for people, there is something radically wrong with us if we are not in solidarity with those who suffer more directly at first-hand. Theological reflection on human suffering is only authentic when in some significant measure it participates in it. When theological reflection on human suffering arises out of solidarity with those who suffer, then the theologian has a distinct and fundamental contribution to make because, as Iulia de Beausobre indicates, the problem goes deeper than its awful symptoms.

After a lengthy survey of the history of religious and philosophical reflection on the reality and excess of human suffering, Schillebeeckx comments: 'Even this survey of human history, in which something of what *humanity* is and means to be emerges, will naturally still be limited – perhaps even "elitist". The voices we hear are of philosophical and religious, Marxist and humanist "thinkers", and not the "suffering multitudes".' 'Yet', Schillebeeckx goes on to say, 'it cannot be claimed that these do not give evocative expression to precisely what is a living experience among all men.'[6] What follows is an attempt to give such evocative expression in relation to our knowledge of God and our own situation.

The Justification of God

Through the centuries many have struggled to unravel the mystery of human suffering in order to justify the apparently unfair and inscrutable ways of God.[7] 'If God is Almighty, and all-loving, why does God permit the birth of a thalidomide baby, the death of a child at the hands of a drunken driver, the cancerous death of a person in mid-life, or the genocide of nations and groups of people through famine, plague, earthquake and flood?' Central to the long and often profound discussion of this theodicy question has been the reality of human freedom, the pervasiveness of evil, the cruelty of nature, and the inevitability of death. At an even more fundamental level, the problem shifts the focus from the Reformation quest for justification before an accusing God, to the justification of God before an accusing humanity tempted, as was Job, 'to curse God'.

No other problem has been so perplexing for believers, or such a stumbling block to those who would believe. Suffering is especially a problem for the person who believes, or who wants to believe in God. Yet, paradoxically, the problem can only be handled from the perspective of faith. This, certainly, is the perspective of the Bible which, as Walter Eichrodt has shown, protests against any theodicy based on rational theory.[8] Pondering upon the problem of the justification of God in the midst of the immense suffering of World War I, P.T. Forsyth concluded that the questions which arise 'are quite unanswerable . . . We can but fall back on the last choice and committal which we call faith.'[9]

The recourse to the language of faith and therefore of mystery may be a way of escape from facing the logic of harsh facts, an irrational, naive response to bolster traditional piety lest it succumb to atheism. We all know that the theodicy question cannot be side-stepped with any such theological sleight-of-hand. Forsyth was well aware of the intellectual problems surrounding suffering and the justification of God. His response of faith was not an escape from rational discussion, nor was it a failure of intellectual nerve. It was the more profound response of a second naivete, the simplicity of biblical faith that sometimes characterises those like Forsyth whose intellectual integrity and grasp is beyond question. For them, atheism itself, however courageous and honest it may be, however much it is the painful rebellion of an Albert Camus against the absurdity of life, does not resolve the problem but rather raises even more serious questions, ending, as it logically must, in nihilism.

Forsyth's recourse to faith is a rejection, on the one hand, of ultimate meaninglessness, and on the other an affirmation that however much we may and must probe the mystery of the ways of God they ultimately remain beyond our intellectual grasp. When the biblical writers struggle with the problem the result is the drama of Job or the powerful and striking metaphors of the prophets. They have a perspective which enables them to make sense of senseless reality, but it is the perspective of commitment and risk rather than water-tight argument. Reflecting on a passage in Dostoievsky's *The Brothers Karamazov*, Schillebeeckx comments: 'Human reason cannot in fact cope with concentrated historical suffering and evil.'[10]

Perhaps it is for this reason that the most satisfying attempts to grapple with the reality of suffering have been those of dramatists, poets and novelists, who like Dante, Dostoievsky and John Milton have explored the theme out of the depths of their own cultural and historical experience. Here too we often find the alienated prophets who speak a word the church dare not ignore. Anyone familiar with black poetry in South Africa, the poetry of a James Mathews, Oswald Mtshali or Mongane Serote,[11] will know that this is true within our own contemporary context. They do not provide rational answers, they may only express deep hurt and anger, yet their passionate grappling with pain is itself a means whereby we can begin to relate to it. Listen to Serote:

> Too much blood has been spilled
> Please my countrymen, can someone say a word of wisdom
> It is too late
> Blood, no matter how little of it
> when it spills on the brain –
> on the memory of a nation
> it is as if the sea floods the earth
> The lights go out
> mad hounds howl in the dark

103

Ah, we've become familiar with horror
the heart of our country
when it makes its pulse
ticking time
wounds us
My countrymen, can someone who understands that it is
    now too late
who knows that exploitation and oppression are brains
which being
insane only know violence
can someone teach us how to mount the wound and fight.
The bright eye of the night keeps whispering and
    whispering
the shadows form and unfold
the trees hide in the dark
the grass whistles
the night is silent with experience
this night
in these parts of the world
... But,
no screams ring forever
nor does pain last forever
something will always be done
the night knows this
this night which makes a day ... [12]

Without denying the importance of rational discussion of
the problem, I suggest that theological reflection on human
suffering has more in common with the passionate explor-
ations of the poets and dramatists than it has with the often
dispassionate debates of the philosophers.

The problem of the justification of God has not grown
any less difficult since Forsyth pondered upon the horrors
of the First World War. Indeed, as the twentieth century
has advanced, the problem has increased in scope and
intensity. Atheism, which since the Enlightenment has

moved beyond the domain of the intellectual elite and become the working creed of the masses, has done so not least because of the experience of the apparent absence of God in the hour of human suffering. The Holocaust, the annihilation of Hiroshima and Nagasaki, the devastation of Vietnam, and the excessive suffering of so many millions due to famine, poverty, racism, war and oppression, have made it very difficult to believe in a God who is both all-loving and Almighty. Moreover, the problem has been exacerbated by the performance of those claiming to be the representatives of God revealed in Jesus Christ, whose calling is to witness to the reality and reign of God.

The Crusades, anti-Semitic pogroms, the Inquisition, the Wars of Religion, the alliance between Colonial conquest and missionary penetration, the Christian sanctioning of the slave-trade and child labour, the 1914-18 conflict between 'Christian' nations, the complicity of German Christians in the Holocaust, the Christian legitimation of racism and oppression in the Deep South and South Africa – such suffering sanctioned by Christians and the church in the name of God have eroded faith in God as much as, if not more than, the intellectual difficulty of reconciling human pain with God Almighty and God all-loving. 'God is dead!' proclaimed Friedrich Nietzsche, 'God remains dead! And we have killed him.'[13]

In a lecture on the situation in Namibia, Gerhard Totemeyer has a very telling paragraph on the position of the church in Ovamboland. 'According to Bishop Dumeni of the Ovambo-Kavango Church' writes Totemeyer, 'the population has reached the limit of human suffering. It is not only the suffering of people he is concerned about but their daily dying as a result of the war. Bishop Dumeni maintains that people are still very much oppressed and persecuted.' Dumeni's 'impression is that whites are not particularly concerned about independence and that if they would have suffered as much as the blacks in Namibia they would have opted for independence long ago. Instead, he says, "the whites are more interested in their economic wellbeing than in human suffering."[14] Such indifference to suffering on the part of those who lay claim to a Christian heritage indicates the extent to which professed faith in the God of Jesus Christ has, in fact, been denied in practice. For all practical purposes, despite protestations to the contrary, such people have become atheists and, in the process, they are forcing the victims of suffering to question whether or not there is a God. And if there is, then, to echo the words of those who taunted Israel: 'where is your God?' (Joel 2:17).

The Whereabouts and Identity of God

The experience of the absence of God, which the Jewish author and philosopher Elie Wiesel and others who lived through the Holocaust have articulated so powerfully in relation to their own historical experience, is much closer to our own doorstep than many of us realise. Consider the poignant, painful and weary cry of Maria Zotwana, an elderly Mfengu woman dumped in the Ciskei.

> 'We had no choice' she said, 'the guns were behind us, then they bring us to this sad place. Here there is not enough food. I am hungry now, as I am sitting here. Everybody has died. My man has gone and died, as have my daughters. They took my land away. The Lord has also gone, yes, I suppose he has also gone.'[15]

The cry of Maria Zotwana, which has been echoed by many others, brings us to the heart of the matter and the focus of this chapter. Her experience of the departure of God, of

106

God leaving her and her community in their hour of grieving and need, derives not from intellectual reflection on the
problem of suffering but from the existential experience of
pain and meaninglessness brought about not just by the
indifference of white Christians, but even more by a policy
which has claimed Christian legitimation.

Two profoundly theological questions arise out of this
suffering and indifference to or even legitimation of it. The
first concerns the whereabouts of God. 'Where is God?'; the
second follows closely upon the first because it is inseparable from it, it is the question of identity, 'Who is God?'
'The biblical question, "Where is God?"', writes Eberhard
Jungel, 'finds its proper *Sitz im Leben* in the struggle for the
right God.'[16]

The first question, concerning the whereabouts of God,
is raised by the experience of the departure, eclipse or absence of God which has led to the growing disillusionment
with Christianity amongst younger blacks, a turning away
from faith to atheism. 'If God is the one in whom whites
believe, then we can no longer believe in God.'

> What I see in Egoli
> are tall buildings
> smart cars
> well dressed people
> a whole scene
> that has no place for me
>   no place for my wife
> no place for my children.
>
> Lord Jesus, where are you?
> Are you in those smart white offices
>   those smart white houses
>   those smart white churches?
>
> They think you are.
> They talk about you the whole time

Just as if you were right there with them.
They are so sure
that you are guiding them,
that they are doing your will.
I like to think
that you are actually here with us
that you are one of the left out ones.

If that is how it is
if you are really here
with us, for us,
I think I could bear it
because I'd know
this wasn't the end,
that you still come
to get prisoners out of gaol
and blind people out of darkness,
to get hungry people into the place
where they can feed their little ones
instead of helplessly hopelessly
listening to them cry.

But my son does not call you Lord,
Jesus,
let alone call on you,
Lord Jesus,
He uses your name as a swearword.
Jesus! he says,
Bloody white man's Jesus!

I fear for him,
for us,
for those whites.

O Jesus, Jesus,
come soon,
clear up the barriers
open it all up, because if you don't
something awful is going to happen.

> Do you hear me,
> one of those 'homeland' blacks
> on the outside looking in?
> RSVP
> soon.[17]

For protest atheism, and that is the kind of atheism we are talking about,[18] human suffering can neither be dealt with by the mystifications of the theologians nor by the rational explanations of philosophers who only seek to interpret the world; human suffering can only be overcome by changing the economic and political structures which are their chief cause.

The second question concerning the identity of God, what kind of God we believe in, is raised because the praxis of those using God to legitimate oppression and suffering, or remaining indifferent to it, contradicts what we know of God revealed in Jesus Christ. It is not a truism that all people who believe in God believe in the same kind of God. By definition, while the Judaeo-Christian tradition posits that there is only one God, it also recognises that there are also many idols, many false images, many misconceptions and misrepresentations of the God whose revelation is witnessed to in the Scriptures. What kind of God, then, encounters us in this witness, and in what way does this kind of God enable us to handle the problem of human suffering?

In this way, then, the theodicy question is raised in a new and radical way for us in South Africa. How can we justify God before an increasingly sceptical and radicalised younger generation who look elsewhere than the Christian faith for their understanding of reality? In fact, as Jungel perceptively shows, 'In this question, "Where is God?", the old questions which dealt with the being and the existence of God have been summarised in a new and unique way.'[19]

'What kind of God?' and 'Where is God' are *the* theological questions of our time; they are also *the* theological questions of our own situation in South Africa.

The Wrath and Grief of God

The experience of the absence or hiddenness of God is expressed in strikingly vivid terms within the Old Testament.[20] In a recent study of the theme, Samuel Balentine shows how prevalent the experience is:

> In the early narratives of the wanderings in the wilderness it is the lack of food and water that prompts Israel to question God's presence. In the complaint psalms it is the experience of unjust suffering which leads the worshipper to accuse God of being capricious in his treatment of his own people. With the prophets the sense of God's hiddenness is identified with his departure from Jerusalem. For the Wisdom writers the hiddenness of God's activities is a problem arising out of the fragmentary nature of human understanding. In one way or another the problem is present in virtually every stratum of the Old Testament.[21]

The experience of the absence of God in the Old Testament is never understood in Nietzschean terms as though God is actually dead. Only the fool, so the Psalmist tells us, believed that. No, the absence of God is not structural but, as Terence Fretheim so perceptively argues, the diminishing of presence.[22]

While some experiences of God's absence are seemingly inexplicable, one reason that is persistently given for God's absence is that he 'hides his face' because of Israel's disobedience. This disobedience and therefore absence of

God is often most apparent when Israel seeks to be most religious on days of prayer and fasting:

> 'Why have we fasted', they say,
> 'and you have not seen it?
>
> Why have we humbled ourselves,
> and you have not noticed?' (Isaiah 58:3 NIV)

But the ultimate expression of such hiddenness coincides with a 'hardness of heart' which darkens and distorts the perception of reality and prevents the people from accepting God's prophetic word of judgment through the prophets. In rejecting the word of the prophets, the people fail to repent and change, and, as a result they have to suffer the inevitable judgment of God which is the withdrawal of grace and the presence of wrath.

> O Jerusalem, Jerusalem,
> you who kill the prophets
> and stone those sent to you,
> how often I have longed to gather your children together
> as a hen gathers her chicks under her wings,
> but you were not willing. (Matthew 23:37 NIV)

Thus the 'wrath of God' which works itself out in history is the ultimate experience of God's absence, of God's distancing himself from and punishing human sin. God is present, but is experienced as one who is no longer gracious, he has lost his patience and has turned his back upon his people. They have deserved their suffering. Instead of God gathering his people together in peace, Jerusalem shall be surrounded by the nations and destroyed in war.

This human experience of God's absence or wrath is integrally related to *God's* own experience of human sin and

111

disobedience. It causes God's grief. Yet it is precisely this grief of God, this pain and anguish which God experiences, which is at the heart of the biblical witness to the character or identity of God. For the Hebrew prophets, as Abraham Heschel expresses it, 'divine ethos does not operate without pathos . . . His ethos and pathos are one. The preoccupation with justice, the passion with which the prophets condemn injustice, is rooted in their sympathy with divine pathos.'[23]

> In all their distress he too was distressed,
> and the angel of his presence saved them . . .
> Yet they rebelled
> and grieved his Holy Spirit.
> So he turned and became their enemy
> and he himself fought against them. (Isaiah 63:9-10)

God suffers because God is holy love. If God were incapable of wrath, of being moved to grief by injustice and oppression, God would not be holy; if God were incapable of suffering, of being moved to grief by the pain and agony of the victims of society, God would not be love. Moltmann rightly shows the connection between the wrath and the love of God when he writes:

> What the Old Testament terms *the wrath of God* does not belong in the category of the anthropomorphic transference of lower human emotions to God, but in the category of the divine *pathos*. His wrath is injured love and therefore a mode of his reaction to men. Love is the source and the basis of the possibility of the wrath of God. The opposite of love is not wrath, but indifference. Indifference towards justice and injustice would be a retreat on the part of God from the covenant.[24]

God grieves, then, because of the rebellion of his people; God grieves because of the broken relationship between

112

himself and his people; God grieves because of the inevitable consequences of human sin and rebellion; God grieves because he remembers what might have been! Thus it is that Fretheim, on the basis of the Old Testament, can speak of 'the wounds of God', the 'parental pathos in the heart of God', the 'mourning of God' and the 'weariness of God'.[25] Or, simply, the 'suffering of God' at the hands of his people. 'If God has opened his heart in the covenant with his people,' writes Moltmann, 'he is injured by disobedience and suffers in the people.'[26] Yet the people of God deserved their suffering. What of the victims of their injustice? What of those who because of the faithlessness of Israel find it difficult to believe in God?

The suffering of God described so poignantly and powerfully in the Old Testament is not just grief caused by a sinful and disobedient people, it is also suffering with and on behalf of those who suffer as a result of Israel's sin – the poor, the oppressed, the hungry, the lowly and innocent ones. 'The human cry becomes God's cry, God takes up the human cry and makes it God's own.'[27] God's apparent withdrawal from his people because of their sin is at the same time a drawing near to those who suffer as a result of poverty and oppression, even though they may not be aware that God is near at hand. Indeed, the heart of God's grief is the fact that those who suffer innocently are sometimes unable to know God's gracious presence in their pain. When Christians cause others to suffer and thereby prevent them from knowing God, the grief of God becomes most intense. Maria Zotwana's cry is what Bonhoeffer called God's 'hour of grieving'.[28]

The Crucified God

The contemporary debate about God raised by human suffering, has emerged largely out of the challenge which the Holocaust and Hiroshima have posed for Christianity. It is, therefore, not unexpected that the first grappling with the theme in our time was done by a German theologian, Dietrich Bonhoeffer, during his imprisonment by the Gestapo, followed by a Japanese theologian Kazoh Kitamori, whose *Theology of the Pain of God* was first published in 1946.[29] Jewish scholars such as Martin Buber, Emil Fackenheim, Richard Rubenstein and Elie Wiesel, have in turn struggled with the significance of Auschwitz for their own faith, and in the process radically challenged Christian theologians. But it was not until 1972, when Jurgen Moltmann wrote his systematic study, *The Crucified God*, that the theme became firmly established as central to the debate about God. The possibility of a future nuclear Holocaust has also led some theologians, notably Gordon Kaufman, to a consideration of what this newly acquired human ability not only to kill millions of innocent victims but to destroy God's creation as such, means for our traditional understanding of God.[30]

It is in this context that we have to understand the resurgence in our time of the concept of the 'death of God'. As Jungel has pointed out, this phrase and the idea it seeks to express has a long and worthy history in Christian tradition, beginning as it does with the Latin Church father Tertullian in the second century.[31] It was later a central theme in medieval mysticism, especially in Meister Eckhart, and then in the *theologia crucis* of Martin Luther.[32] Although certain developments in the Christian debate about the 'death of God' derive from Nietzsche, for Bonhoeffer, Kitamori, Moltmann and Jungel the point of departure is Luther and

114

the tradition which he restated so powerfully in his time.

For Nietzsche, God *is* dead! For the Christian theologian from Tertullian to Luther to Jungel, this is an absurdity because if God is God he cannot die. Yet, at the same time, the cross is a reality for God, something really happens to God or the whole event is a sham. God experiences in himself the ultimate suffering of his own wrath and absence; he takes upon himself the pain and suffering of the whole creation; God becomes the defenceless victim. And thus it is, according to the gospel, that God can only be known through his suffering and weakness revealed in Jesus Christ. On the cross God is most intensely present and absent; grace and wrath are most powerfully at work.

It is understandable that reason reacts so violently against this notion of a suffering God, and why patripassionism (the suffering of God the Father) was rejected by the patristic theologians. But patripassionism is not the issue here, because we are not talking about the same kind of suffering. We are talking about suffering love, and as we have already established a God who is unable to suffer is unable to love and clearly not the God described in the Bible.[33] Dorothee Soelle is correct when she writes: 'Atheism arises out of human suffering. A God who senselessly torments in death a woman who has dedicated her life to him cannot exist. To be sure, the faith that disintegrates in this experience is a theism that has almost nothing to do with Christ.'[34] The God who suffers is not the God of popular theism; such a God has nothing to do with the crucified Christ. It is a different *kind* of God. Thus the protest of atheism brought about as a result of suffering, excessive, innocent, oppressive suffering, forces us to reconsider not the question of God's existence but God's essence.[35] As both Jungel and Moltman show, the alternative to the atheist protest against a God who permits innocent, oppressive

115

suffering is not a theism which tries to defend the defenceless, but a trinitarian understanding of God who is a participant in our suffering.

In the same way, Takatso Mofokeng in *The Crucified
Among the Crossbearers*, the most thorough attempt to
develop a black Christology in South Africa to date, speaks
of the cross as 'a trinitarian moment'. This does not resolve
the problem of human suffering, but it does provide a perspective within which it can be handled. 'The screams of
God-forsakenness in history remain and even increase.'
Yet, on the cross, Jesus fully identified with human suffering even to the extent of the pain of being abandoned by God.

> On the cross the Father, in a unique actualisation of his
> love for man in the world of extreme opposition to him, gave
> his son fully and completely to do that which is sufficient in
> ending the centre of the power of his enemies. It is therefore
> no wonder that Jesus, the son, screamed the scream of God-
> abandonment. This is the scream of those with whom he
> identified and for whom he suffered. They feel, above the
> pain inflicted by their torturers, the excruciating pain and
> agony of suffering in God-abandonment at the moment
> they would most need him, i.e. his intervention. In this, he
> was indeed like us in everything. But now in Jesus' case, and
> here lies the difference, he experiences God-abandonment
> doing justice, suffers injustice in total obedience to his
> Father! Here he is not like us and we are not like him. In fact
> he calls us to be like him and to do justice to the very end.[36]

This lays the basis for our own crossbearing, our own participation in the struggle for justice as disciples of the crucified.

Dietrich Bonhoeffer saw a direct link between this *theologia crucis* and our contemporary experience of God's absence which has resulted from the process of seculariza-
tion. In his letter of 16 July 1944 from Tegel prison,

Bonhoeffer wrote these well-known words:

> We cannot be honest unless we recognize that we have to live in the world *etsi deus non daretur.* And this is just what we do recognize – before God! God himself compels us to recognize it. So our coming of age leads us to a true recognition of our situation before God. God would have us know that we must live as men who manage our lives without him. The God who is with us is the God who forsakes us (Mark 15:34). The God who lets us live in the world without the working hypothesis of God is the God before whom we stand continually. Before God and with God we live without God.

It is this understanding of the presence and absence of God, neither being possible without the other, that leads Bonhoeffer beyond the question 'where is God?' to its inseparable companion, 'who is God?' But even more, to the question to which we must now turn, 'How can such a God help us in our suffering?' Thus this moving passage on the suffering of God:

> God lets himself be pushed out of the world on to the cross. He is weak and powerless in the world, and that is precisely the way, the only way, in which he is with us and helps us. Matt. 8:17 makes it quite clear that Christ helps us, not by virtue of his omnipotence, but by virtue of his weakness and suffering. Here is the decisive difference between Christianity and all religions. Man's religiosity makes him look in his distress to the power of God in the world: God is the *deus ex machina.* The Bible directs man to God's powerlessness and suffering; only a suffering God can help.[37]

The question that then has to be faced is precisely *how* does the suffering God help us in our suffering? How does God's grief move beyond solidarity in our pain and become redemptive?

117

Participation in the Suffering of God

According to the Old Testament, the intensification of God's suffering inevitably results in a fresh breaking forth of creative and redemptive activity.

> The period of restraint is a time of ever-intensifying labour pains for God, which finally burst forth in the travail of the emergence of a new creation. This birth-event, however, will entail not simply the emergence of a new people of God; the act of re-creation will affect the whole world (Deut. 32:15-16). God, crying out, gasping, and panting, gives birth to a new order. The new creation *necessitates* the suffering of God.[38]

In other words, the transformation of the human situation requires the suffering of God.

How does God suffer redemptively in the world? Once again the Old Testament points the way forward. God's redemptive suffering is embodied in those who serve him faithfully. In the profoundly moving final chapter of his book, Fretheim shows how this embodiment reaches its height in the Old Testament in Jeremiah and the Suffering Servant of Second Isaiah. They not only proclaim God's suffering, they embody it in their lives. The people do not simply reject their prophetic word, they actually reject and persecute them. Thus the way is prepared for the total and unique embodiment of God in the Word become flesh, the crucified Messiah.[39]

Two days after Dietrich Bonhoeffer had written to Eberhard Bethge about the powerlessness of God he wrote a further letter from prison in which he referred to a poem he had previously written. He wrote:

> The poem about Christians and pagans contains an idea that you will recognise: 'Christians stand by God in his hour

118

of grieving'; that is what distinguishes Christians from pagans. Jesus asked in Gethsemane, 'Could you not watch with me one hour?' That is a reversal of what the religious man expects from God. Man is summoned to share in God's sufferings at the hands of a godless world.

Further on, Bonhoeffer continued:

It is not the religious act that makes the Christian, but participation in the sufferings of God in the secular life. That is *metanoia*: not in the first place thinking about one's own needs, problems, sins, and fears, but allowing oneself to be caught up into the way of Jesus Christ, into the messianic event, thus fulfilling Isa. 53.[40]

It is on this basis that we can then begin to think of the witness of the church in the world, not just as the bearer of the Word but as depicted in I Peter: 'participating in the sufferings of Christ' (4:13 NIV). God's redemptive suffering in Christ becomes concrete in the world through the life and witness of the suffering community of faith and especially its prophets. Without this embodiment the message of the cross remains theory, an empty word that reinforces the experience of the absence of God amongst those who suffer injustice and oppression. The ultimate failure of the People of God, whether it be Israel in the Old Testament, or the Christian church, is when it becomes the cause of such suffering instead of the suffering servant which mediates the redemptive love of God. The followers of Jesus vicariously endure suffering on behalf of others; they do not inflict it on them. Suffering becomes redemptive when it is vicarious, and in our context that only becomes possible when we accept our guilt in the suffering of others and our responsibility to be in solidarity with them. In this act of solidarity we meet God and discover not only *where* God is but also *who* God is.

119

Thus the message of the suffering God, the word of the cross, requires a fundamental change, a *metanoia*, in the self-understanding of the church in our time. It especially requires fundamental change on the part of white Christians in South Africa, for we have been responsible for so much of the pain and anguish of others. The church under the cross is the church which suffers vicariously on behalf of those who suffer at the hands of the powerful. This means that the *theologia crucis* has to be understood in relation to the society in which we live. In this regard, Moltmann rightly perceives the socio-political significance of the *theologia crucis*:

> In political terms, its limit lay in the fact that while as a reformer Luther formulated the *theologia crucis* in theoretical and practical terms against the medieval institutional church, he did not formulate it as social criticism against feudal society in the Peasant Wars of 1524 and 1525. What he wrote to the peasants did not express the critical and liberating force of the cross, the choosing of the lowly which puts the mighty to shame, nor the polemic of the crucified God against pride and subjection, domination and slavery, but instead a non-Protestant mysticism of suffering and humble submission. The task therefore remained of developing the theology of the cross in the direction of an understanding of the world and of history. The theology of the cross had to be worked out not merely for the reform of the church but as social criticism, in association with practical actions to set free both the wretched and their rulers.[41]

This is what Metz calls the 'dangerous memory of the passion of Christ' which challenges and transforms society.[42] It is precisely at this point that prophetic theology relates directly to human suffering, for it sets the problem within the context of social forces and approaches it both theologically and in terms of social analysis.

Traditionally the problem of theodicy has been resolved by positing an after life in which the unjust inequities of life are redressed. Such an 'eschatological resolution'[43] may or may not be adequate for the problem as traditionally formulated, but for those who suffer oppression and injustice *now* it sounds too much like a legitimation of the status quo in the name of God. If, however, we shift the focus to the church as witness to the passion of God then the theodicy problem is lifted from the realm of abstraction to that of historical concretion, from the realm of the intellect to that of praxis. Only in this way can we meet the most challenging critique of faith in God today in our situation, which is derived from Feuerbach and Nietzsche and most powerfully expressed in Karl Marx, namely, that God is an illusion created to enable the oppressed to handle their suffering, and the corollary, God is an invention of the powerful and rich to justify their self-interests and therefore to justify the suffering of the powerless and poor.

Thus it is that Nicholas Lash, in the concluding chapter of his theological reflections on the thought of Karl Marx in *A Matter of Hope* relates the question of God to that of the witness of the church:

> The character of the question of God is (I would say) only appropriately exhibited by strenuous engagement – in action, prayer and suffering – in the work of transforming the circumstances of human existence.[44]

The Christian response to the problem of oppressive suffering thus becomes participation in God's transforming action in the world, an action which is both historical and concrete. That means engagement in the struggle to end injustice and to point towards the coming of God's kingdom. To return to Mofokeng's discussion of Jesus' cry of dereliction from the cross:

121

With his cry on the cross, he raises new followers. He also calls his followers who had abandoned him at this decisive hour, the poor, the sick and the sinners and the disciples who had distanced themselves from him or fled from him to follow him to the very end, even the end of the cross. He calls them to take that ultimate action, like him, to endure torturing and crucifixion for justice and fraternity and triumph because he has triumphed as his resurrection reveals.

Mofokeng continues, bringing his volume to its climax:

Their Christian existence as a life in faith, love and hope shall be a militant one against anti-Christian forces and structures that are opposed to the emergence of the poor and the oppressed as inheritors of the earth and of a human community of equals. Their faith shall be a faith against the destruction of faith, their love shall be love against hatred and bitterness, and their hope in the coming of the new society shall be a 'hope against hope'.[45]

There is a profound sense in which black theologians like Mofokeng and liberation theologians like Gustavo Gutierrez are saying that the church is, in fact, most truly comprised of those who are poor, oppressed, and therefore of those who suffer.[46] In other words, the church is not simply the community of Christ which suffers vicariously for others, but the suffering church is also the victim of oppression. Moreover, many within this suffering church are engaged in the struggle for their liberation from oppression, and doing so as Christians. Thus, in South Africa, where the vast percentage of Christians are from the 'underside of history', and where many of them have been forced by circumstances to engage in political struggle, we have to re-think the identity of the church. There is already a suffering church in our midst, a church of the victims who are also struggling for justice. A suffering church which is crying out to those of us who are privileged and who think we

122

are the church, to hear the Word of the Lord, a word which certainly is one of judgment, but also a word which carries within it our hope. Or is it so, that the church of the privileged in South Africa and elsewhere has become, like Israel of old, 'hard of heart' and unable any longer to 'hear the things that belong to our peace'? Is this why prophets are persecuted, because they challenge us and our values?

For many blacks in South Africa, especially but not only those who are in the forefront of the struggle for justice and liberation, it is not so much God who is beyond belief, but the church which has lost its credibility. Indeed, if God has become a problem it is precisely because those who claim to believe in God have too often denied him in practice. The credibility of the church's testimony today is bound up not so much with its intellectual ability to defend the faith, to solve the theodicy problem as traditionally stated, though I do not underestimate the importance of that, but far more with the willingness of the church to participate in the sufferings of Christ for the sake of the world. And this means to share in the struggle for justice. To be sure, the justification of God can only be resolved eschatologically, but that takes place penultimately in history through authentic witness to the kingdom of God.

The God in whom we believe, the God revealed in the crucified Messiah, the God who is present even when he is experienced as absent, and absent when we think he is present, this God has opted to be on the side of those who suffer because of the oppression of others. God always takes this option according to the Scriptures because he is the God of justice. But God suffers on their behalf in order that the rest of us may come to *metanoia* and thereby also know his grace in his wrath and experience the redeeming power of the cross. God's grief brings us to repentance. Christians are certainly called to 'stand by God in his hour of grieving', but over and above our meagre attempts to participate in God's suffering, as Bonhoeffer went on to say in his poem 'Christians and Pagans', is God's presence in our suffering, waiting and wanting to forgive and redeem those who turn to him in humble trust.

> Men go to God when they are sore bestead,
> Pray to him for succour, for his peace, for bread,
> For mercy for them sick, sinning, or dead;
> All men do so, Christian and unbelieving.

> Men go to God when he is sore bestead,
> Find him poor and scorned, without shelter or bread,
> Whelmed under weight of the wicked, the weak, the
>   dead;
> Christians stand by God in his hour of grieving.

> God goes to every man when sore bestead,
> Feeds body and spirit with his bread;
> For Christians, pagans alike he hangs dead,
> And both alike forgiving.

The minister of the Word of God is always a witness to the vicarious suffering of Jesus Christ, his act of redeeming solidarity on behalf of humankind. 'We preach Christ Crucified' declared St Paul. But this proclamation of the crucified God Incarnate, is not an idea but an historical event which becomes concrete through the Spirit in our context. Thus Paul 'dies daily' in being crucified with Jesus Christ, truly witnessing to the redemptive power of the cross. It is this vision, this power in weakness which should direct not only the pastor and prophet but the whole people of God, for it proclaims who God is and where God is to be found.

CHAPTER FOUR

The Theological Formation
of the People of God

Thus far we have considered the vocation of the ordained ministry as a calling to be a practical theologian within the community of faith. By this is meant that the ministry of the Word and Sacraments exists to enable the church to discover its direction for mission in the world, a task which is at once pastoral and prophetic. We have now set this task within the context of oppressive suffering and the particular challenge which this presents to the church and its mission in South Africa. In this final chapter we shall explore the vocation and tasks of the ordained minister as practical theologian engaged in the theological formation of the People of God. A formation which enables the community of faith to become a prophetic community in word and deed, and therefore not only one which shares in solidarity with those who suffer but also struggles alongside them for justice.

Our focus in this chapter will be on the traditional roles of the ordained ministry within the life of the church, but we shall examine them in the light of our understanding of practical theology and the ministry and mission of the church as a whole in the world. Focusing on such traditional roles as preaching, pastoral care, and liturgical leadership, derives in part from the conviction that such tasks remain central to the vocation of the ordained ministry. They are moreover fundamental to the theological formation of the People of God and its equipping for mission. Such traditional tasks, however, like all traditions, can be taken for granted, pursued uncritically, and become unrelated to or even counter-productive for the mission of the church in the world. They are too important, however, to allow them to be jettisoned in some 'radical' attempt to restructure the church, or to become the property of those who, in the name of preserving the church and Christian faith, really want to maintain an unjust status quo and prevent the church from relating in a liberating and transformative way to the context and crises in which it finds itself. Traditional tasks, like the symbols of the Christian tradition itself, need to be reappropriated in ways consonant both with their original intention and the needs of the present context.

In examining the traditional roles of preaching, pastoral care, and liturgical leadership, we must, of course, see them in relation to the life and ministry of the church as a whole and not as a clerical preserve. For this reason we shall only consider them once we have reflected upon the task of the lay theologian, or the theological vocation of the People of God as a whole. Furthermore, because our concern is not primarily that of technique, whether in preaching, pastoral care or liturgical leadership, but rather orientation, we will begin by providing a perspective within which the 'how to' tasks of ministry should be considered.

Practical Theologians or Clerical Technicians?

Most of us who have been educated in the secularizing traditions of the Enlightenment tend to think in mechanistic terms about the world. Despite modern developments in physics which call this Cartesian and Newtonian worldview radically into question, we still operate on the basis that the world functions like a vast machine. In *The Turning Point: Science, Society and the Rising Culture*, Fritjof Capra, himself a renowned scientist, provides us with a trenchant criticism of this tradition which has become so all-pervasive in our modern world, especially but not only in the West. By way of example, Capra focuses his attack especially on much modern medicine and the pharmaceutical industry. These, he argues, treat human beings as though we are machines rather than persons. Unlike more traditional healing, they accept a radical dualism in which mind and spirit are separated from the body. The aim is not to enable wholeness but to repair part of the physical machinery which has malfunctioned. In this way, hospitals and even surgeries have become the human equivalent of garages or motor service stations. Contrary to this, Capra writes, 'modern physics has transcended the mechanistic Cartesian view of the world and is leading us to a holistic and intrinsically dynamic conception of the universe,'[1] and therefore of the human being and of society.

Capra's critique of the way in which Cartesian dualism and Newtonian physics has affected our worldview, is widely shared by contemporary theologians.[2] In *Liberating Creation*, for example, Gibson Winter has argued that the crisis facing modern society is a struggle between two root metaphors, the mechanistic with all its destructive power, and the creative with its holistic vision of reality.[3] Throughout what follows this distinction should be kept in mind because it is essential for re-stating the task of the ordained ministry.

Consider the following observations which Fritjof Capra makes in comparing machines and organisms, thinking of them by analogy with the church and the ministry. Machines, Capra reminds us, are constructed, whereas organisms grow and are process-oriented. 'Whereas the activities of a machine are determined by its structure, the relation is reversed in organisms – organic structure is determined by processes.'[4] As a result, organisms have a 'high degree of flexibility and plasticity', which enables them to change and adapt to new circumstances. Machines, on the other hand, can only function in a pre-determined, causal way. Moreover, whereas machines are controlled from beyond themselves, 'a living organism is a self-governing system, which means that its order in structure and function is not imposed by the environment but is established by the system itself.'[5] In other words, while organisms interact continually with their environment, that interaction does not determine their identity. At the same time, and this is quite crucial, living organisms 'are open systems, which means that they have to maintain a continuous exchange of energy and matter with their environment to stay alive.'[6] Indeed, they can only live if they learn to adapt to their environment. Related to this is the ability of living organisms to renew themselves, to heal injuries or broken parts, and to reproduce themselves so that even death does not prevent the continuity of life.

The Pauline image of the church as 'the body of Christ' is clearly an organic one. Yet many of us are so influenced by the Enlightenment and its mechanistic worldview that we tend to regard the church also as a machine made up of separate parts. The ordained ministry thus becomes one of servicing the institution in order to enable it to function properly. Instead of being practical theologians ordained ministers become clerical technicians; instead of their focus being on the mission of the church in the world, it is on church maintenance. Indeed, a failure to perceive the church as a living organism, or, to use systems-theory language, an 'open system', and therefore relating to it as a machine, ends up with ministers trying to run the church, maintain it, revive it, and restructure it. Often congregations like this approach because it lets them off the hook. They do not have to be the People of God engaged in theo-

logical reflection and mission. This is tied up with the per-
vasive individualism which also derives in large measure
from the Enlightenment and which is so destructive of
genuine community and therefore of the church. Joseph
Hough and John Cobb refer to this when they write:

> The internalisation of Enlightenment individualism by
> Christians has deeply affected the understanding of the
> church as well. It has also caused some serious problems for
> the concept of the people of God in mission. Individuals do
> 'join' the church, but because American churches, regard-
> less of their official polity, function as voluntary associa-
> tions, they are mostly congeries of consenting individuals
> whose commitment to the church is very conditional.[7]

A successful ordained ministry, working within this
paradigm, is thus one which results in a well-run church, a
high-tech church if you like, but not a congregation of the
People of God that can function without its clerical
mechanic. At worst, such a ministry becomes manipulative
to the extent that those within the church who have spiritual
insight and creative ability withdraw to exercise their
ministry elsewhere. The living, creative energies and gifts
of the Spirit which should flow through the body and constantly renew it are stifled, and eventually the organism
dies. In the process, the ordained ministry as a theological
vocation and integral part of the body likewise expires,
perhaps quite literally through being burnt out.

One symptom of this mechanistic model is the fact that
practical theology is so often reduced to training in clerical
techniques. Instead of being biblical reflection on transforming prophetic and pastoral action involving the People
of God as a whole, practical theology is given an inferior
place in the theological curriculum as something not quite

theological nor academically respectable. Moreover, since the 'how' question is often dealt with in an uncritical manner, it can result in consequences which are highly questionable. Reflecting on theological education and the functionalist/technician paradigm which governs so much of it, Edward Farley puts the matter quite sharply: 'practical theology is increasingly vulnerable to the accusation that it is ordered toward the maintenance of middle-class religion.' Theological education of this kind, he continues, 'perpetuates maintenance roles of clergy in the culture and as such legitimates the structures that encapsulate social oppression'.[8] Clerical technology reinforces both the ecclesiastical and the socio-political status quo because it is designed for maintenance not personal and social transformation.

There is, of course, a great deal written today about practical theology which, while being erudite and scholarly, is anything but of practical help. The 'how' question has been forgotten in the interests of more foundational issues. Compare this to the approach of Dietrich Bonhoeffer in training theological students at the illegal Finkenwalde Seminary during the Third Reich. 'Unlike the traditional preachers' seminaries, in which only the practical aspects of ministry were taught in a technical-school setting, Bonhoeffer' we are told, 'wrestled theologically with his students in order that they might confront the impact of the theology of the Word on pastoral work.'[9] As can be seen from his lectures on pastoral care, Bonhoeffer did not exclude instruction on 'how to' fulfil the tasks of ministry; on the contrary, Bonhoeffer was quite explicit and detailed in this regard, but he always did so on the basis of theological reflection and insight. Knowledge of 'how to' preach or attend the dying is not to be disparaged. We can all learn a great deal from those who speak from years of faithful pastoral experience. But to reduce the ordained ministry to the level of a clerical technician designed to maintain the institution is to destroy the vocation of preacher, teacher, pastor and prophet.

There is another consequence. The biblical vision of the church is not only that of a living organism, but also of the People of God participating in God's transforming purposes in society. In the past it has generally been true that an organic view of reality results in a conservative, hierarchical and even authoritarian understanding of society and the church. However, this need not be so if an organic approach is related to a theology of the kingdom of God which has to do with social and personal transformation. Indeed, if the church as the prototype of the new humanity perceives itself in mechanistic terms and functions as a machine, then it also perceives society in the same way and shapes its mission to the world accordingly. We thus end up with a missiology which is manipulative, trying to control rather than serve people and society, and often only perceiving others in individualistic and statistical terms.

An attendant danger is that the holistic character of mission is lost. Nicholas Wolterstorff, reflecting on the thought of Abraham Kuyper and the social witness of the church, writes: 'Only if we once again see society not as a heap of souls on a piece of ground, but as a God-willed community, as a living human organism, can there be any cure to the misery of poverty.' It is interesting, given the generally conservative character of Kuyper's thought and the way in which it has been misused in South Africa, that Wolterstorff continues: 'And that, says Kuyper, is "the socialist path".'[10] It is not only the church which needs to be understood in organic terms but society as a whole and, for the Christian, they are organically related to each other in Jesus Christ.

131

Lay Theology: Peoples' Theology

In the first chapter we distinguished between academic, practical and lay theologians, and referred to the different publics or arenas within which they function. We also insisted that while they are different in their focus they should always remain interdependent because they ultimately share the same concern. There, however, we only dealt with the tasks and relationship of the academic and the practical theologian. But just as theology is not the sole prerogative of the academic, neither is it the prerogative of the ordained ministry. Indeed, when theology remains within the domain of the 'professionals' it can be counterproductive for the mission of the church.

Stephen Sykes in *The Identity of the Church* reflects at length on the role of professional theologians in the life of the church and the power they exercise in shaping its identity. His concluding paragraph is germane not only to our immediate concern but to the chapter as a whole:

> Theologians ought not to conceal from themselves, or from others, the power which they undoubtedly exercise in their interventions in the life of the Church. But neither, on the other hand, ought they to arrogate to themselves the power which belongs properly to the community as a whole, that of preserving the identity of Christianity by means of committed participation in the Church's worship in word and deed.

Mindful of the academic debates which many theologians get into and how these unnecessarily and adversely affect the life of the church and its mission in the world, Sykes continues:

> The processes of internal argument ought never to come to predominate over the achieving of the Church's major

tasks. While there can be no convenient moratorium in these disputes during which the Christian community may put its house in order, every participant in an internal conflict ought to have regard to the mobilisation of resources for the infinitely greater external struggles in which it is involved. The theologians' commitment in those larger battles is determined, with that of the Christian community as a whole, by that worship which longs for the coming of God's kingom.[11]

There are and have been many excellent lay theologians. I am reminded of Bernard Lord Manning of Jesus College, Cambridge, a Congregational layman earlier this century whose writings certainly had an impact upon me as a student.[12] Manning's comment: 'When we can botanise about the Burning Bush, either it has ceased to burn or it has been consumed', remains pertinent with regard to much academic theology; it is also, I fear, true of much preaching and teaching.[13] But not all lay theologians are of the intellectual calibre of a Manning, Dorothy Sayers or C.S. Lewis. To be a lay theologian does not mean being an academic any more than this is necessary for the practical theologian. Rather, what is at stake here is the development of theological insight or discernment within the community of faith in the context of daily life, worship and witness, and the theological formation of the *laos* within its historical context.

Every Christian is called to be a theologian. Gustavo Gutierrez reminds us of this in the opening paragraph of his *A Theology of Liberation:*

> Theological reflection – that is, the understanding of the faith – arises spontaneously and inevitably in the believer, in all those who have accepted the gift of the Word of God. Theology is intrinsic to a life of faith seeking to be authentic and complete and is, therefore, essential to the common consideration of this faith in the ecclesial community.

> There is present in *all believers* – and more so in every
> Christian community – a rough outline of a theology.[14]

While this might appear to undermine the contention that
theology is the vocation of the ordained ministry, it really
affirms it. The ordained ministry exists to enable the community of faith to reflect theologically on its life and witness
in the world in order that its members may better understand their faith, calling and task as Christians in the world.

The relationship between the ordained minister as practical theologian and the theological formation of the People
of God is not a one-way matter. Lay people bring to the task
of theological reflection insights and expertise which are
usually beyond the knowledge and experience of the academic or the pastor. Thus the theological formation of the
People of God includes as part of the process the theological formation of the ordained ministry. Though there is
always a need for highly or at least well-trained theologians,
both in the academy and the community of faith, clericalism in the guise of the expert theologian has no place at
all. Indeed, the theological vocation of the ordained ministry can only be fulfilled within the life of the Christian community as it struggles to be the People of God in the world.
It is within the grid of life that practical theology is born. As
Gutierrez goes on to say, the faith and witness of the community of believers provides 'the soil into which theological
reflection stubbornly and permanently sinks its roots and
from which it derives its strength'.[15]

Many newly ordained ministers well-versed in academic
theology discover, sometimes the hard and often embar-
rassing way, that there is more theological wisdom in their
congregations than in what they managed to digest in seminary. Or at least this is potentially the case, providing that
their predecessors did not suppress the gift of theology in

the congregation. In this regard we do well to ponder the words of F. Ross Kinsler, the Presbyterian missionary who pioneered theological education by extension in Guatemala:

> The institutions and structures that have evolved in Europe and North America can no longer presume to hold the keys to theological understanding, prophetic insight, or spiritual vitality. Genuine spiritual, prophetic, and theological life emerges from the basic church as 'ordinary' Christians engage in their daily vocation. The task of theological education is to release, not bypass or supplant, that source of life and power.[16]

Perhaps it is for this reason that John Cobb says: 'it does not make sense to me to teach students a system from which they can then minister. It does make sense to encourage them to think seriously as Christians about the real problems of the church.'[17] This reinforces the argument that theological education must be integrally related to the theological formation of the church as an organic whole, and therefore to the mission of the church in the world.

We can learn a great deal about this from what has been done in and achieved through theological education by extension (TEE), not least within the southern African context.[18] But this does not present us with the final word on the subject of theological education today. Indeed, it is noteworthy that Hough and Cobb in their programme for theological education, while noting the importance of TEE and other alternative forms of theological education, nevertheless affirm the importance of the seminary and underline what we previously noted about the inter-relationship between the academic and practical theologian:

> Alternative congregationally-based education, and education by extension, do indeed enlarge the opportunity for

reflection in action, but they sacrifice the immense value of seminary-based practical reflection on professional action, particularly the kind of reflection which must be based on continuing biblical, historical, and social-scientific research. The congregation simply does not provide the setting, time, or resources for the disciplined study required for professionals who will lead the Christian community in its search for an adequate contemporary expression of its identity along with reflection on authentic concrete Christian practices in its world-historical context.[19]

Hopefully it is self-evident that in talking about the theological formation of the People of God we are not talking about some kind of theological dilettantism on the part of either the pastor or congregation. There may be a place for this in a university extra-mural programme, and there are occasions when curiosity about divine things may have unexpected consequences. 'It will always be well for men to understand' wrote Karl Barth, 'that the question with which they turn to us is far more radical than in the random perplexities of life they have imagined it to be'.[20] Human curiosity often hides a more profound searching for truth and understanding, so that even the apparent idle question can open up possibilities for genuine theological reflection and personal transformation.

But quite apart from anything else, I am convinced that the layperson, and by no means only the Christian believer, is hungry for genuine theological insight. As Daniel Jenkins wrote some years ago in his assessment of religion in England:

> The extraordinary public interest aroused by Bishop Robinson's *Honest to God*, in itself a modest essay in theological restatement, suggests the presence of a deep, unsatisfied hunger for theological illumination.[21]

But it must be stressed that this hunger will take different forms in different cultures, as well as in different social and political contexts. The hunger for meaning and the thirst for righteousness and social justice belong together. But whatever its form, such hunger and thirst is constant to the human condition. It is the concern to make some sense out of life, suffering and death.

In the intervening years between *Honest to God* and the present, as the crisis of faith and the struggle for justice has intensified in our world and respective societies, this deeply human hunger for meaning and understanding has neither disappeared nor subsided. It has rather become acute in situations of massive suffering, poverty and oppression. Thus whereas in some more stable and affluent contexts the theological formation of the People of God may take place within a relaxed atmosphere where traditional themes can be explored at leisure and at will, in other contexts the theological formation of the People of God has to take place in the midst of crisis, social uncertainty, repression and resistance. The theological formation of the church is in such situations not primarily the satisfaction of the hunger for insight and understanding, but enabling the community of faith to discover its direction in the world as witness to the gospel of the kingdom of God.

Lay theology in such situations becomes not the theology of lay people who are sufficiently well-educated to understand the argument of an *Honest to God* or *The Myth of God Incarnate* or whatever may be their most contemporary equivalent, but what is now referred to as a 'peoples' theology'. By this is meant a theology which arises out of the shared experiences and reflection of that segment of the People of God who live in situations of poverty, oppression and suffering. Oft quoted examples of such theology is that of the 'base communities' in Latin America, or Minjung

Theology, or the theology of some of the African indigenous churches, or the theology of *The Kairos Document* which, in its Preface claims to be 'a peoples' document'. In South Africa, the vast majority of the People of God, or members of the church, happen to be black, the victims of racism and injustice, and are often very poor: a peoples' theology is one which relates to their situation, indeed, one which arises out of their response to the gospel within their particular oppressive context and which, in doing so, challenges the theology of the whole church.

The well-worn cliche, 'theology from below' as distinct from 'theology from above' is often used to distinguish between this kind of theology which arises out of the experience of those who are below in the social structure, and that which comes down from some authority above inevitably wedded to another more dominant social class. Although this is an important distinction it is a misunderstanding of what is traditionally meant by the phrase 'theology from above'. Normally a 'theology from above' refers to a theology which takes as its point of departure the Incarnation, the 'Word become flesh', the divine breaking into our history 'from above'. Theology 'from below' refers, on the other hand, to a theology which begins with the 'Jesus of history', or with our own experience of reality.

But as we have already seen in the first chapter in discussing the Incarnation as the basis for doing theology, these are false and misleading antitheses. A theology worked out from within the experience of an oppressed people can, indeed, be a theology 'from above', a theology which appropriates the liberating power of the Incarnate Word and refuses to allow it to become captive to the interests of those who would use such a theology to legitimate oppressive power. Moreover, a theology 'from below' can easily become, as it did in classical liberal Christianity, the

138

justification of bourgeois and middle-class religion. What is required is a theology which arises out of an understanding of the Incarnate Word within the life, fate and suffering of the one who identified fully with the poor and the oppressed, Jesus Christ. And, therefore, a theology which is at once a genuine 'peoples' theology' because it relates directly to their context of oppressive suffering, and a theology of the People of God as a whole. Wherever the People of God is struggling seriously with what it means to be disciples of Jesus Christ in relation to its context genuine theology is born.

The false separation of theologies 'from above' and 'from below' leads to a further misunderstanding of a genuine theology of the People of God and a 'peoples' theology'. That is, it lends weight to the idea that preaching and teaching the Word of God has to be rejected in favour of articulating the agonies and struggles of the people as they seek to throw off the yoke of their bondage. But a 'peoples' theology', or an authentic liberating and transforming theology of the People of God, is not a theology sundered from the proclamation of the Word. It is a theology which arises out of an encounter with that Word within the context of oppression as the church commits itself to the struggle for justice and genuine reconciliation. It is a Word which addresses the church as a whole because it comes with a new prophetic urgency and directness. In such situations the Word of God truly becomes a two-edged-sword, a word of judgment and liberation, of wrath but also of grace and hope.

The Proclamation of the Word

The practical theologian is a preacher and teacher of the Word of God. Through such proclamation men and women come to believe in and trust God revealed in Jesus Christ; through this ministry of the Word, the community of faith is built up in faith, hope and love; through this ministry the prophetic Word of judgment is announced and the call to seek justice is proclaimed; and through this ministry the People of God in each place discerns the purposes of God for its mission in the world. Theology itself is not revelation, but the practical theologian as minister of the Word of God is a witness to and an interpreter of revelation. As such the task of the minister of the Word is to enable people to know God in Jesus Christ as saviour and Lord, and thereby become disciples of the kingdom of God in witnessing to that faith amidst the struggle for what is right and just in the world. All of this is fundamental to the theological formation of the People of God. As Karl Barth perceived, the proclamation of the Word, whether by preaching and teaching or by witness and action in the world, is central to the existence and identity of the church.[22]

The ministry of the Word can, of course, be reduced to techniques in rhetoric, homiletics and education which are designed to capture and keep an audience. Once again, it is not that technique is unimportant. Few of us who, as theological students, were helped by W.E. Sangster's *The Craft of the Sermon* can deny that.[23] Likewise many of us are indebted to educational methods which have enabled us to be better teachers. But what really made an impact upon some of us as theological students trying to preach sermons was not *The Craft of the Sermon* but James Stewart's *Heralds of God* and P.T. Forsyth's *Positive Preaching and the Modern Mind*.[24] For them, preaching arose out of theological reflection and conviction; its aim was the transformation of people through an encounter with the truth of the proclaimed Word. 'The Christian preacher' wrote Forsyth, 'is not the successor of the Greek orator, but of the Hebrew prophet.'

140

The orator comes with but an inspiration, the prophet comes with a revelation. In so far as the preacher and prophet had an analogue in Greece it was the dramatist, with his urgent sense of life's guilty tragedy, its inevitable ethic, its unseen moral powers, and their atoning purifying note.[25]

In similar vein, Allan Boesak in his essay on 'Relevant Preaching in a Black Context' reminds us that 'Preachers derive their authority not from the people, nor even from the church. They derive it from the One whose word they may proclaim.' Boesak goes to speak of the 'miracle' or 'mystery' of preaching in which 'God speaks to his people through the words of a mere human being.'

Herein lies the truth that the sermon is neither the prattle of pious-sounding words, nor a well-structured oration. The sermon is an event, and again not because of the preacher, but because of the truth that is authenticated in the proclamation of the word. God wants to use a mere human being, not an angel, to proclaim his word, and this causes acute embarrassment in the preacher.[26]

Christian preaching understood as an event means that through the proclamation of the Word the meaning and transformative power of the gospel becomes clear and evident within the life of the community of faith. Hence the insistence of Calvin on the inseparable relationship between the Word and the Spirit, and more recently Peter Stuhlmacher's insistence that biblical interpretation must 'be carried on theologically in regard for the enduring hermeneutical relevance of the Third Article of the Apostles' Creed'.[27] This does not mean that historical biblical scholarship has no role to play in preaching and teaching. Whatever its limitations, the historical-critical method remains important in preventing both preacher and teacher from

141

indulging in flights of interpretative fancy. But the proclamation of the Word is a charismatic event in which text
and reality come together, faith is born or strengthened,
theological insight emerges and the community of faith
whether unschooled or learned discovers its direction for
mission. The task of the minister of the Word is to facilitate
this process through a knowledge of the Scriptures and the
tradition of faith, and an understanding of both the character of the community of faith and its social situation. The
ordained minister is meant to be a charismatic leader in the
true sense: called and gifted by God.

Several questions inevitably arise both for the scholar
and the agnostic, as well as the believer, at this point. What
do we mean by 'the Word of God'? Do we equate it with the
Bible, and, if not, what is the relationship? If the Bible contains the Word of God or, better, is our primary witness to
it, as I would contend, how do preachers and teachers
themselves come to discern and proclaim it today? Is it
not true that however exalted a view we may have of the
ministry of the Word, our own assumptions and precon-
ceptions inevitably affect its proclamation? What is the
relationship between this proclaimed Word in Scripture
and the tradition of interpretation through the centuries
which has become embodied in symbol and liturgy, creed
and confession, and a variety of other denominational con-
tainers? Any attempt to deal with questions such as these in
detail, vital as they are, is beyond the scope of this volume.
Thus much of the ensuing discussion will proceed on
assumptions that are not discussed here.

There is, however, another set of questions which is
more immediately germane to our theme of ministry in context and crisis. Preaching, like pastoral care and the other
responsibilities of ministry, has to be contextual if it is to
retain its basic character as an event in which text and real-

ity come together. As we have already intimated, in South Africa ministry has to be undertaken in ways appropriate to the different life-situations of the black and white congregations. This applies as much to preaching as it does to pastoral care. It is not that the message of the gospel is different, but that the gospel addresses us in terms which relate to our particular context. Clearly this was the case in the ministry of Jesus himself who, in proclaiming the good news of the kingdom, addressed pharisees and prostitutes, centurions and zealots, rich and poor people, in different ways.

The questions we have to ask are therefore such as these: How is the ministry of the Word in preaching and teaching related to the task of theology as critical reflection on the existence and social praxis of the church? How is it to be related concretely to the life and task of the community of faith in the world in each place at a given time? How is preaching to become a prophetic Word addressed to a particular situation? These 'how' questions are not primarily those of technique, but of theological approach. They are fundamental to the task of the practical theologian, bringing us directly to what is now universally referred to as the discipline of hermeneutics (the science of the interpretation of texts).

Unfortunately the debate about hermeneutics has, because of the very complexity of the issues at stake, become highly abstruse. This has led at least one Biblical scholar, Leander Keck, to comment that 'valuable as the study of hermeneutics is in clarifying what has happened when a text has been interpreted, I cannot rid myself of the suspicion that better hermeneutics does not necessarily lead to better interpretation, but the reverse.'[28] Keck goes on to speak specifically about preaching and teaching in a way which relates to our theme:

143

> If one thinks of the great interpreters of Scripture, in any case, one thing seems to emerge: for them there was something self-evident about the text. Whence came that sense of self-evidentness?

He answers:

> In a word, I suspect that vital interpretation occurs either when the interpreter discovers him-or herself placed between a text and reality, neither of which can be surrendered but must be squared (as when liberal Protestants could not give up either the text or modernity), or when he or she discerns a significant reality through the text.[29]

Keck's scepticism about the value of much modern hermeneutical theory for the preacher and teacher derives from the fact that it tends to become an end in itself, a game which scholars play. Rather than exposing the meaning of the text, allowing it to exercise its transformative power, it overlays it with impenetrable theory. But this does not imply that hermeneutics has no place in biblical interpretation. After all, the moment we begin to interpret Scripture for today we are immediately involved in hermeneutics even if we never use the word. The only question is whether it is helpful or unhelpful in the ministry of the Word.

A way beyond the abstractness of the hermeneutic debate in the interests of the ministry of the Word and the formation of the community of faith lies in the manner in which Juan Luis Segundo has restated Rudolf Bultmann's 'hermeneutic circle'. Segundo lifts it out of the realm of philosophical enquiry and places it at the service of the transformative mission of the church in the world. This provides the link between our previous discussion on the pastoral-circle and our present focus. Segundo's definition of the 'hermeneutic circle' occurs in the opening pages of *The Liberation of Theology*. He writes:

It is the continuing change in our interpretation of the Bible which is dictated by the continuing changes in our present-day reality, both individual and societal. 'Hermeneutic' means 'having to do with interpretation'. And the circular nature of this interpretation stems from the fact that each new reality obliges us to interpret the word of God afresh, to change reality accordingly, and then to go back and interpret the word of God again, and so on.[30]

Thus we can speak of a 'pastoral-hermeneutic circle' in which the interpretation of Scripture plays a crucial role. The ministry of the Word of God in preaching and teaching is central to the 'moment of theological reflection' in which the community of faith seeks to discern the will of God in relation to its life and witness.

In all this we have to keep in mind the four moments in the pastoral-hermeneutic circle which we described earlier. The theological formation of the people of God is by no means a purely kerygmatic or didactic event, as though preaching and teaching unrelated to the witness and social praxis of the community of faith is adequate. On the contrary, preaching and teaching are part of the circle, directing and informing witness and praxis according to the Word of God and, in turn, being shaped by the struggles and failures of the church in seeking to be faithful to the kingdom of God in the world. *Theological formation is therefore a dynamic process in which the ministry of the Word of God, witness and praxis, theological reflection, and an understanding of the historical context interact.*

The New Testament letters, especially those of Paul, are marvellous examples of this process whereby a community of faith is theologically fashioned. Paul's letters are full of proclamation *(kerygma)* and teaching *(didache)*, both of which are deeply rooted in theological reflection and insight *(phronesis)*. But this is always expressed in relation to the experiences and issues which perplexed and challenged the churches, and which hindered their pastoral and missiological tasks. In this way, the apostle, working as a practical theologian, enabled these congregations to understand the meaning of their faith and discover its implications for their common life and mission in the process. Some of the greatest theological writings in the history of the church, such as Augustine's *City of God* or more recently *The Barmen Declaration* have come into being in a similar way. Several documents emerging from the church struggle in South Africa, such as *The Message to the People of South Africa*, the Belhar Confession of Faith and, most recently, *The Kairos Document*, may be regarded in a similar way even though we may not give them the same status.

Theological insight often arises out of struggling with the meaning of Christian faith at critical moments in the life of the church, moments when the Biblical tradition and its symbols come alive with new transforming power. But the process should be going on all the time in the regular life of the church, otherwise congregations remain theologically dormant and undirected in their pastoral practice and mission. This is part of the significance of developing the 'pastoral-hermeneutical circle' as a consciously adopted method of theological formation and pastoral practice in which the normal work of the ordained ministry in preaching, teaching, pastoral work and worship are not unrelated, disjointed activities, but an integral and decisive part of the process. Theological education thereby becomes a dynamic process. It involves the whole community of faith in its journey through time and its location in society, as well as its relation to the tradition in which it stands and its present responsibilities within the world. The alternative usually adopted, if anything at all is done, is a didactic programme thrust upon the congregation from outside or even by a well-intentioned pastor, which takes no account of either the particular context or character of the congregation.

The ministry of the Word, especially understood as teaching, must also be set, however, within the larger canvas of historical tradition. In other words, the process through which a particular congregation goes in theological formation for mission is, itself, only part of a much larger historical project, a project which encompasses the People of God as a whole and many different traditions within it.

Over the past few years some biblical scholars and theologians have rediscovered the narrative character of theology, a character that suffered, in Hans Frei's words 'an eclipse' in eighteenth and nineteenth century hermeneutics.[31] Thus Stanley Hauerwas speaks of the need for the church today to become 'a society shaped and informed by the truthful character of God we find revealed in the stories of Israel and Jesus' in order to discern what obedience means, of what God's will for us is today. He writes:

> The remarkable richness of these stories of God requires that a church be a community of discourse and interpretation that endeavours to tell these stories and form its life in accordance with them. The church, the whole body of believers, therefore cannot be limited to any one historical paradigm or contained by any one institutional form. Rather the very character of the stories of God requires a people who are willing to have their understanding of the story constantly challenged by what others have discovered in their attempt to live faithful to that tradition. For the church is able to exist and grow only through tradition, which – as the memory sustained over time by ritual and habit – sets the context and boundaries for the discussion required by the Christian stories.[32]

The practical theologian as preacher and teacher plays a crucial role in this process and therefore needs to know not only the content of the story, but also the way in which it should properly be told, received, critically evaluated and appropriated in new historical contexts. Or, to put it in other words, how the community of faith can become consciously, yet critically, a part of the tradition in a new time and place in such a way that its mission to the world has direction derived both from hope and expectation and also from its cumulative memory and experience. Included in this is an ability to relate the particular tradition within which the community of faith stands to the ministry of the Word today in preaching and teaching, as well as in worship. This task requires all the theological resources of the academy and the church, as well as the experience and insight of the community of faith as a whole.

The Retrieving of Tradition

Many Protestants have an inbuilt suspicion of the word 'tradition'. For them it means that Scripture is subject to ecclesiastical control, the whims of men, and the vagaries of history and custom. The fear which gives rise to such suspicion is not unfounded. 'The traditions of men', as Jesus perceived, can so easily prevent the inbreaking of the living, prophetic Word. Yet, despite the claims of some that they are able to preach and teach the Bible alone, it is inevitable and necessary that this takes place within some tradition of interpretation and practice. It is far better to acknowledge this and deal with it properly, than to assume that it does not apply to or affect one's own position.[33] Protestants have become as much captive to their traditions and their cultural determinants as anyone else. Thus today for example, Christian feminists or black theologians raise searching questions regarding the cultural captivities of mainstream church tradition, and contemporary iconoclasts, as in the past, reject tradition as beyond redemption and call us to start again.

At the same time tradition is a biblical concept which has to be taken seriously. We speak of the Biblical tradition because we are aware that Christian faith does not exist in a vacuum but is historically mediated. It is something which is handed on to us, something which we take up in the present, and points us to the future. For this reason David Tracy uses the expression 'the Christian fact' because, as he says,

> the word 'fact' serves to remind us that Christianity is not something we invent. Christianity exists and demands rediscovery and interpretation – the latter including retrieval, and critique and suspicion – but not invention.[34]

Christian tradition is the story of faith to which we have already referred, which begins with Abraham, the story of the People of God journeying through history in response to the call and grace of God. The Biblical and the historical tradition that arises out of it, despite all its wanderings and apparent contradictions, is a story of faith finding expression in confession, in words and symbols, in Torah and apostolic teaching, in liberating action and reconciling deed.

Christian tradition is thus properly understood as a cumulative, organic process of continuity and discontinuity within which the contemporary People of God stand, and within which theological reflection and praxis takes place. Christian tradition is misunderstood if it is conceived in mechanistic terms, as though it is simply embodied, for example, in synodical resolutions or pipe-line theories of ordination and the like. Historical tradition is rather a living reality that continues the narrative of the Bible, a process of formation of the People of God under the guidance of the Holy Spirit. In fact, *theological formation in the Biblical and historical tradition is the awakening of an historical consciousness, an awareness of who we are as the People of God, and what faithfulness to Jesus Christ and the message of the kingdom of God requires of us today.*

The problem of the relationship between Scripture and tradition, including the relationship which is made in ecumenical discussions between *the* apostolic tradition and traditions, is a complex one. Edward Farley speaks of Scripture and tradition as '*vehicles of ecclesial process* by means of which the originative event of Christian faith is able to endure as normative and to function redemptively in the transformation of human existence.'[35] But clearly this does not mean that we can equate denominational traditions with *the* Christian tradition, nor can we assume that the latter is itself uniform rather than diverse in character.[36]

Furthermore, while the Bible must remain normative we have to acknowledge that the Bible itself contains diversity of tradition and that this is partly the reason for plurality within the Christian tradition. From the earliest times there were already different traditions in the life of the church rather than a universal orthodoxy or orthopraxis.[37] Hence Henrikus Berkhof's trenchant comment:

> It would not be difficult to describe church history as a history of conflicting and antagonistic interpretations. And it would be quite well possible to view the whole as history in which the divinely upsetting power of revelation is suppressed and rendered innocuous by misinterpretation and conformism. For the most part it can be described as the history of the successive and simultaneous Hellenisation, moralisation, Germanisation, nationalisation, scholastici-

sation, and liberalisation of the gospel. Think of what men like Kierkegaard and Franz Overbeck said about church history! The true history of the church has mostly been the history of lone individuals, martyrs, and minorities.[38]

This conflict in the development of Christian tradition is not necessarily bad because tension can be creative, and 'traditions, when vital, embody continuities of conflict', Alisdair MacIntyre rightly notes.[39] Nonetheless, it is still possible to talk about the Christian tradition as a historical reality, as a process which contains a diversity of sometimes conflicting but often complementary traditions.

While, on the one hand, the theological formation of the People of God must be ecumenical and catholic, on the other hand, this does not mean a denial of the particular trajectories in Scripture which have become embodied within particular historical traditions. On the contrary, as Rosemary Radford Reuther reminds us:

> It is impossible to be objectively universal, that is, to include concretely all human groups, all historical traditions, all perspectives in one's theology. To claim to do this is simply to set up an abstract ideology in which a new, perhaps enlarged, particularity claims to be the universal, but actually excludes many people, many traditions, in a way that renders them invisible.[40]

Each of us lives and works within the context of a particular tradition of Christian faith which shapes our understanding of the gospel and the church. These particular traditions have sometimes emerged within the church as the body has sought to renew its life. But by their very nature they have invariably been partial in their expression of the truth, and therefore in tension or even conflict with each other. Genuine particularity, as we have insisted before, is how-

151

ever not antithetical to universality but can contribute to it by sharing insights derived from a different historical experience and perspective. This is especially true when those who live within a particular tradition are able to retrieve elements within it which are not only open to the commonality of Christian faith but which also contribute to the ongoing transformation of the church and society. It is not a question of some fundamentalist regurgitation of the tradition, but of retrieving that which gave it life, embodying it in a new time and place, and so making it universally available.

There are, however, traditions which have closed in on themselves, made their own interpretation of the Christian fact ultimate, and so cut themselves off in principle from any attempt to reach a commonality of faith with those of other traditions. They fail to recognise that they too have been shaped by culture and social forces rather than unmediated revelation, that they too are particular and not sufficiently universal. We have usually identified such traditions as sectarian, but we need to remember that sectarianism is a mind-set found throughout the church which cuts the body off from resources which can contribute to the renewal of its life. For this reason it is always important to recognise that while 'tradition furnishes the stream of conceptions within which we stand', we need to 'distinguish between fruitful presuppositions and those that imprison and prevent us from thinking and seeing' beyond ourselves.[41] Thus Edward Farley:

> Theological understanding would be incomplete, even self-destructive, if it failed to apply a hermeneutics of suspicion to its own tradition. For what in fact is tradition? Even if it is granted the status of revelation, divine disclosure, it is something which occurred in the historical past. In other

152

words, the tradition and its imagery, primary symbols, and dogmas originated in former concrete *situations*. In whatever sense it is divine work, it is clearly also a human work. To grant it the status of the eternal itself is clearly one more idolatry.[42]

Such idolatry becomes crystal clear when a particular tradition is wedded to a specific culture as, for example, Calvinism has been wedded to Afrikaner nationalism in South Africa, and English Christianity to British imperialism. This reduces the tradition to an ideology with disastrous consequences not only for Christian faith and the life of the church, but also for society.

Theological reflection within the community of faith has, then, the task of being ever critical of the tradition in which it stands. But the intention of such critique is not only the overcoming of false moves previously made. It is even more the retrieval of vital elements from the tradition and its reconstruction in the contemporary context. In Gregory Baum's words, the purpose of the ideological self-critique by those within a particular tradition is

> to regain the positive symbols of their tradition that produced life and vision in the past and that could, in a new key, generate the ideals for a new social order ... What counts in any reform movement – or any revolution, for that matter – is to reinterpret the significant images and symbols that people have inherited and thus regain them and reclaim them as sources for a new social imagination and guides for a new kind of social commitment.[43]

Thus the practical theologian, at that moment of theological reflection in the pastoral-hermeneutical circle, draws on the insights and symbols of the tradition in order to help the community of faith find its way. In particular, the practical theologian reappropriates those symbols in the tradition which communicate the liberating and transforming power of the gospel of the kingdom of God in Jesus Christ.

In South Africa we may think especially in this regard of the Reformed tradition and the way in which it is being critically examined and re-appropriated in a new liberating way, not least through a re-examination of the Biblical message.[44] Scripture remains normative in this process of deconstructing and revitalizing Reformed tradition. Nicholas Wolterstorff, speaking from within it puts it tersely and in a way which applies equally to other traditions:

> There is yet one more path toward the goal of becoming self-critical, and indeed, it is the most direct of all: it is the path of listening attentively to the prophetic word of the Bible, that great unmasker of self-deceit.[45]

Yet, as his book demonstrates, the Bible is an unmasker that also points the way forward for the People of God.

It is precisely in this way, living out of an historical tradition and retrieving elements within it that need to be appropriated for today, that new possibilities for the future open up for the church. 'An adequate sense of tradition,' Alisdair MacIntyre writes, 'manifests itself in a grasp of those future possibilities which the past has made available to the present.'[46] Theological reflection plays a crucial role in this process as the French Protestant philosopher, Paul Ricouer, reminds us: 'the main task of theology' is to 'return us to the primary understanding of a tradition with fresh possibilities for it becoming a transforming reality in our lives.'[47] Reformed theologians, for example, when true to their tradition know very well that an 'appeal to tradition has been historically one way of opening up the future to change, even to revolution'.[48]

A vital part of the responsibility of the Reformed or other theologians in South Africa today, at least in seeking to be faithful to their particular tradition is, then, radically to question the way in which the tradition has distorted both itself and the Biblical tradition, and to retrieve those elements within it which open up fresh possibilities for faithful witness today. From a Roman Catholic perspective Matthew Lamb says precisely this when he writes of 'the need to express our solidarity with the victims of the past by not surrendering the traditions to those in power'.[49] 'It is not a question of compromising the religious scriptures and religious traditions in order to "apply" such watered-down versions of religious teachings to social and political struggles. Rather it is a question of showing how those human struggles for freedom reveal the true meanings and values of the narratives and teachings of religion.'[50]

Much of the foregoing discussion may seem remote from the daily life and vocation of the ordained minister. In fact it is not, because the pastor or priest is the one who represents and interprets the Christian tradition, or a particular variation of it, within the life of the congregation. Often this is done without much awareness of either the problems or the transforming potential of the task, and often the ordained minister bcomes trapped in traditionalism or, in breaking free, becomes captive to some passing fad. There is the need, then, to show how this process is applicable to the life of the ordained minister as pastor and liturgical celebrant, and how it relates in this way to the theological formation of the People of God.

Pastoral Practice and the Christian Tradition

The relationship between pastoral practice and theological formation in an historical tradition can be illustrated if we return to our earlier discussion on the relationship between pastor and prophet in the life of the church. Robin Gill is misleading when he writes: 'The priest within the church is concerned with building up a moral community, whereas the prophet (often at loggerheads with his church) is more concerned with radical social change.'[51] What Gill states may be a description of what is often the case, but it is certainly not what should be true. Both priest, or pastor, and prophet should be representing and interpreting the same tradition, so that the building up of the community of faith and obedience on the basis of the Christian tradition is integral to the transformation of society and vice versa.

One of the most significant books to be written on pastoral theology in recent years is Don Browning's, *The Moral Context of Pastoral Care.* Browning's main concern is to counter the influence which non-evaluative, non-directive forms of secular therapy and counselling have had upon pastoral care. The pastor is not a secular therapist in clerical disguise, but a practical theologian who has a responsibility for the care of people committed to a particular historical tradition and project. For Browning, the pastoral ministry loses its identity and purpose when it operates outside the moral values and commitments of the Judaeo-Christian tradition. Pastoral care and prophetic ministry share a common foundation, vision and goal, and they can only fulfill their respective tasks in the theological formation of the People of God as they relate creatively to each other. Thus Browning writes: 'Pastoral counselling must be founded on a context of moral meanings that is, in fact, the province of practical theology.' And, again, 'It is the minister's primary task to help establish and maintain the moral vision of the worshipping community and the wider society.'[52]

This understanding of the wholeness of Christian ministry in which pastor and prophet alike share in the same historical tradition and commitment to the coming kingdom of God is important because it recognises the significance of the historical context within which pastoral care takes place. Pastoral care is both rooted in an historical tradition and related to personal and social transformation in a particular historical context. While the phrase 'cure of souls' has a long and venerable history, it is misleading if we think of souls in some kind of disembodied way. Pastors do not care for people in the way a mechanic may care for the parts of an engine. Souls are people living in particular social contexts, and they cannot be understood let alone cared for except in relation to their context.

Take, for example, pastoral care within the South African context. Pastors who really seek to minister to the needs of their congregations at this time of social crisis know that they have to take very seriously the fears, expectations, tensions, mistrust and general sense of despair which are endemic to the situation. Moreover, they know that these will vary greatly from one community to another, and that pastoral care within a black township will invariably be different in this regard from that in a white community. The history of pastoral care, told by John T. McNeill in *A History of the Cure of Souls*, shows how it has been shaped by changing contexts and crises in both church and society. 'Religion, in short, cannot be dealt with in a vacuum. Although it may possess its own unique structures and institutions, their particular manifestations reflect and in turn influence all other aspects of culture.'[53]

Pastoral problems are often related directly to social

context even if they are not caused by it. While the break up of a marriage may have nothing ostensibly to do with the surrounding culture, most perceptive pastors know that cultural norms and pressures play an enormous role in affecting human relations both within and outside the home. This became very clear to us in South Africa during the social unrest in 1985. What were ostensibly personal or interpersonal problems were sometimes caused, or at least made more difficult and complex, by the socio-political crisis. But this is not only true in societies where crisis is more obvious and endemic. Langdon Gilkey, writing in a North American context says much the same thing:

> in addressing *our* anxieties as Christians in church, we are in fact discoursing on our wider culture's problems. If we would understand our personal crises, therefore, we must as theologians understand also that wider structure; if we would speak a healing word to personal problems, we must envision new possibilities for our cultural history.[54]

Western Europe or North America may not be going through a social crisis in the same way as South Africa is, but they are not less societies in crisis. Their crisis, which is largely the result of rapid secularisation, is, as Alisdair MacIntyre, has so powerfully argued in *After Virtues,* the collapse of values and meanings which have somehow given society its sense of cohesion in the past.

Even more significantly, perhaps, the failure of the church to minister generally to the working class or, at least, the failure of the so-called mainline churches to do so, is indicative of a lack of ability to relate pastoral practice to questions of labour and socio-historical forces.[55] Once again, it shows how serious it is when pastoral care is not grounded in a genuine practical theology. This means also a practical theology which has an informed awareness of social and cultural forces, and is therefore in dialogue with the social sciences in so far as they enable social analysis.

Pastoral care is not much help if, as is the case with so many secular therapies, it simply reinforces the values of a social milieu. On the contrary, as Browning argues, 'it is being recognised increasingly that value conflicts and value ambivalences are themselves a major cause of problems in living and in even the more severe forms of mental illness.'[56] This being the case, pastors are not helping those for whom they care by 'protecting' them from the moral and spiritual challenges of the gospel, on the contrary this contributes to the problem and prevents them from discovering the resources available in the tradition. Genuine pastoral care enables discipleship and growth in Christian maturity. 'Spiritual care', Bonhoeffer told his students at Finkenwalde, 'does not want to bring about competence, build character, or produce certain types of persons. Instead it uncovers sin and creates hearers of the gospel.'[57] The danger of 'cheap grace' is that it prevents people from experiencing real grace in their lives, and so becoming disciples engaged in transforming praxis.

If pastoral care does not take place within the context of the genuine theological formation of the People of God, then it prevents rather than enables mission. 'An organic sense of *style* – of the way "we people are"', writes Browning, is fundamental if a community of moral discourse is to become a community of action.'[58] Christian pastoral care is not intended simply to resolve personal problems, vital as this is, but to do so in such a way that those who are being helped and healed are in turn enabled to participate in some way in evangelism and the transformation of society.

Thus the pastor should take care that the People of God are able to respond positively to prophetic witness, not reject it. Prophetic ministry, as Walter Brueggemann puts it, 'consists of offering an alternative perception of reality and in letting people see their own history in the light of God's freedom and his will for justice.'[59] It is true that there will always be prophets in the mould of Amos who do not fit easily into the ecclesiastical structures and mould of the day. Yet it is also true that the church itself should not fit easily into its cultural milieu; it too is meant to refuse to conform to the world, and thereby be a community of salt, that is, a social irritant that heals. If this be so, then it is not only the prophets but also the pastors who, perhaps in different ways and at different levels, have the responsibility 'to nurture, nourish, and evoke a consciousness and perception alternative to the consciousness and perception of the dominant culture around us'.[60] Pastoral care is about the 'cure of souls', but it is also about the creation of a prophetic disciple community.

An important distinction must be drawn, however, between a pastoral ministry which is prophetic and one that is moralistic. In stressing the need for pastors to operate within the context of the Judaeo-Christian tradition, and especially its tradition of moral and ethical values, Browning speaks to this issue: 'How to enter into sensitive moral inquiry with troubled and confused individuals without becoming moralistic is,' he contends, 'the major technical and methodological task for training in pastoral care in the future.'[61]

Theologically, this means that while grace is always costly and never cheap, it is nevertheless always grace, and grace, while always ethical, is never legalistic or moralistic. A moralistic ministry, whether expressed in preaching or pastoral care, keeps people in bondage to their failures, sins and guilt, and thus prevents them from responding in obedience to the word of the prophets and the call of Christ to discipleship.

Pastoral care is meant to be a means whereby people discover the grace and forgiveness of God and experience the healing and renewing power of the Spirit, in order that they may follow Christ in obedience. For this reason we have to see pastoral care not only in relation to the prophetic and ethical dimensions of the Christian tradition, but also in the context of its traditions of spirituality and doxology. The theological formation of the People of God is a process which takes place not only, nor even chiefly at the level of critical reflection; it takes place also, and perhaps above all, in the context of worship.

Liturgy, Theology, and Hope

The Christian community is a community of worship and praise. As the Eastern Orthodox tradition never ceases to remind us, theology is doxology. This does not mean that theology is therefore not a scientific enterprise, rather it places that task within a context which is not simply one of rational, academic discourse. Scientific theology is a necessary task. It is the task of rigorously examining and expressing the Christian tradition in relation to present contexts and crises; the task of dethroning idols in the life of the church and society; the task of evaluating the praxis of the church in the struggle for social justice. But all of this is done for the sake of more truly knowing and serving God, the God revealed in Jesus Christ. For this reason we may say that the ultimate goal and test of theology is not understanding the Christian faith better, but knowing and loving God better.

The knowledge and love of God is never separate from the mission of the church in the world. The prophets constantly remind us that 'to know God' means 'to do justice', and 'to love God' implies loving our neighbour and our enemy. Thus the theological formation of the People of God is the enabling of a community to express such praise of God in the midst of the world. True doxology then rejects any false dualism between spirit and matter, between spirituality and involvement in political struggle, between the sacred and the secular. True doxology affirms that the whole creation belongs to God and that the goal of all creation is the praise of God.

In *Doxology: the Praise of God in Worship, Doctrine and Life*, Geoffrey Wainwright provides us with some useful insights into what it means to do theology in such a liturgical perspective. Firstly, he insists that the theologian should pursue his or her task within the worshipping life of the Christian community set within the wider context of the human community. Secondly, within this context, rather than the academy or university, the theological formation of the People of God takes place. Thus both the task of the theologian and the theological formation of the People of God find a focus in the context of the liturgy: the preaching of the Word, the eucharistic celebration; the fellowship, praise and prayers of a people engaged in serving the world.

In the opening chapter of *Doxology*, Wainwright describes the task of the individual theologian, a task that applies pre-eminently to the practical theologian in the life of the congregation. He writes:

> It is the Christian community that transmits the vision which the theologian, as an individual human being, has seen and believed. As a believer, the theologian is committed to serving the Christian community in the transmission and spread of the vision among humanity. *Worship* is the place in which that vision comes to a sharp focus, a concen-

162

trated expression, and it is here that the vision has often been found at its most appealing. The theologian's thinking therefore properly draws on the worship of the Christian community and is in duty bound to contribute to it.[62]

Even though those of us who do theology in contexts of more overt oppression may wish to inject different content into our theology than that which is to be found in Wainwright's more traditional, first-world exposition, nevertheless what he says enables us to see more clearly what the practical theologian should be about. It is not only as pastor and prophet, but also as liturgist that the ordained minister is a theologian. Indeed, in the liturgy it all comes into focus as the Word is proclaimed, the bread broken, and the community offers itself in prayer for the service of the world. This is the moment above all others when theological reflection happens.

Liturgy, like the word tradition, has had a bad press in many Protestant circles and has only recently and reluctantly been accepted. This is because liturgy has been confused with ritualism and formalism, with a form of worship in which the freedom of the Spirit is excluded in principle. Much liturgy has been guilty of this. It has become mechanistic, and the role of the liturgist has been perceived as that of a technician. But we have come to recognise that even what we call free church worship can be as formalistic and spiritless as the most structured and ritualistic, and the apparently most free order of worship can be the most manipulated by clerical technicians. While the structure of the liturgy is important, what makes a liturgy come to life in genuine praise of God is not primarily its structure but the spiritual authenticity of the worshipping community as a living organism. Many of us can testify to the fact that we have been encountered by the reality of God in very diverse liturgical settings, and in similar settings been struck by the

163

lack of that presence. Fortunately, God has the happy ability to break into the liturgy of all traditions and create his own dynamics either in unison with the liturgy or in opposition to it.

In view of what we have already discussed concerning the church as an organism rather than a machine, it is interesting that Wainwright uses the notion of open systems as an appropriate way to consider theology and the life and worship of the church in the world. Open systems theory, as Fritjof Capra shows, is central to our understanding of living organisms. Wainwright relates this to a proper understanding of the liturgical life of the church:

> My belief in open systems is both grounded in and confirmed by my experience of Christian liturgy, with its stable structures that give room for improvisation, its regularities that allow adaptation to circumstance, its familiarities that permit the new to be recognised. Biologically, a closed system is moribund if not quite dead; yet the vital openness can be predicated only of a cohesive system. Spiritually, life and thought require both order and freedom for their flourishing.[63]

If liturgy is understood in this way, then it becomes the way in which the People of God week by week become aware of the historic tradition in which we stand and the call of God to relate that tradition, in word and deed, to the context in which we live. An essential and integral part of the theological formation of the People of God has to do, then, with participation in a liturgical life that makes theological sense and helps develop theological wisdom.

There is great theological insight embedded in the classical liturgical traditions, and if these are used properly as vehicles of the Spirit, then they can and do play a major role in shaping the life, convictions and commitments of the community of faith.

Indeed, the reappropriation of the liturgical traditions of the church in such a way that the liberating and transforming symbols of faith and the gospel communicate afresh in our present context, is vital to the shaping of the character of the Christian community and its mission in the world. If this does not happen, the liturgical traditions turn inward, stagnate, and deny their original intention through becoming vehicles of conservation rather than transformation. The alternative is not, of course, worship which is trendy and captive to the needs of the moment.

The essential element in all worship is surely that of transforming encounter with the living God in praise, prayer, the preaching of the Word and the sacraments, in such a way that our lives are renewed by grace and sustained by hope. Writing as a sociologist, Robert Bellah aptly described worship as that which facilitates 'the experience of the holy', but he also spoke of forms of worship which 'become a defense against that experience'. He continued

> If the traditional rituals often attempted to bind the power of the sacred into a compulsive pattern that acted like a neurotic symptom, the modern debasement of worship into moral edification devoid of the power of the holy is not adequate either.[64]

Likewise, when a liturgy has no theological substance, coherence and direction, it not only inhibits theological insight and understanding, but reinforces misconceptions about Christian faith and discipleship. It can also reinforce social attitudes which are contrary to the gospel. A theologically bad liturgy projects a false image of God, of ourselves, and of the gospel, and thereby prevents the birth and growth of true theological insight and ecclesial praxis.

Moreover, bad liturgy is also remote from the cultural experience of the people at worship, and therefore unrelated to their 'language', their specific needs and hopes. Hendrikus Berkhof, who has some very fresh and illuminating things to say on the life and worship of the Church, brings both these dimensions together when he writes:

> Tradition, customs, cultural level, and particular needs vary a great deal according to geographical area and historical period, making for a great diversity in possible and legitimate liturgies. That does not, however, do away with the underlying fixed structure of the liturgy. The encounter character of the meeting (i.e. the service of worship) implies both variability (God regularly encounters different people) and a certain stability: the point is always the encounter with the same God whom we come to know in Christ through the Spirit. The liturgy is to structure the encounter and therefore must itself be structured as encounter.[65]

The ordained minister together with other leaders within the congregation has a special responsibility to ensure that the liturgical life of the congregation involves the whole People of God, does so in relation to their context, and facilitates their theological formation. 'We *must* find a way,' Bishop John Robinson wrote, 'each according to our own tradition, of letting the action speak; we must allow the structure of it, "the shape" of the Liturgy, to stand out.'[66] Robinson had the fourfold eucharistic action particularly in mind, but it is equally true that the whole of worship as well as each facet, whether it be the preaching or the selection of hymns, the prayers, baptism, or the way the eucharist is celebrated, needs to be shaped and used with this in mind.

In the celebration of both sacraments there is a powerful opportunity for the retrieving of the gospel tradition and its contemporary restatement. The celebration of baptism, like the celebration of the eucharist, is intended to be a highly symbolic action and, according to the Reformers, to communicate what it signifies. The pastor as practical theologian should regard baptism as a particularly important moment in the theological formation of the People of God. Its coupling of God's grace and the call to costly discipleship, together with its rich meaning as the sacrament of unity through which people of all races, classes, cultures, as well as 'male and female', are brought together as equal members in the body of Christ, presents a unique opportunity for the proclamation of the Word in symbolic action.

Nowhere else than in the proper celebration of the eucharist, which includes the faithful proclamation of the Word, do we, as the People of God, see more clearly or participate more fully in the tradition which relates us to the central events of our faith and which, in turn, opens us up to the future of the coming kingdom of God. Nowhere as much as in the eucharist is the false separation of the material and spiritual transcended, as bread and wine become a means of grace. Moreover, in the breaking and sharing of the 'body of Christ' we are meant to become partakers in Christ's redemptive action in the life of the world, sharing the bread of life which alone meets the deepest human needs, but also sharing our bread with the hungry and working for the transformation of their material situation which keeps them poor and deprived. Thus, nowhere else is hope so central, the hope which refuses to accept the present disorder and which longs and works for the coming of God's justice and peace.

The time has surely come when we who are in traditions where the eucharist is not celebrated week by week as an integral part of worship need not only to recognise that this is a serious flaw, but also to remedy the situation. This alone, as Nicholas Wolterstorff so rightly argues, 'is the decisive step that must be taken if we wish once again to have a balance of worship and proclamation – if we wish to overcome the tragedy of liturgy in Protestantism.'[67] It was, after all, the Protestant Reformers who insisted that Word and Sacrament belong together, and none other than Calvin who insisted on the weekly celebration of the Lord's Supper.

It is not for nothing that worship and spirituality have been discovered anew by those engaged in the struggle for justice in the world. This has been as true in Latin America as it is true in South Africa. Of course, very many have been so alienated from the life of the church that they have rejected not only the church and worship, but also belief and hope in God. Indeed, political atheism, which is sometimes the product of false religion and a reaction to the attempt to give Christian legitimacy to oppression, is rife within our context, and understandably so. But it is also true that many who are militant for justice have discovered the reality of worship and prayer in a new way.[68] 'To accept this possibility', writes Nicholas Lash, is 'to acknowledge the function of liturgy indirectly to contribute to the liberating transformation of prevailing social conditions and social consciousness . . . the *Christian* evocation of the 'sacred' will be an evocation of that which transcends our present inhumanity.'[69]

At the heart of the liturgy is the prayer of Jesus, the prayer which reaches its climax in asking that God's kingdom 'may come on earth as in heaven'. Similarly, at the Lord's Table, we celebrate the death and resurrection of Jesus Christ 'until he comes'. The theological formation of the People of God is a formation which is open-ended, a formation which can never reach completion until the 'kingdoms of this world become the kingdom of our God and of his Christ'. The theological task is always *in via*, en route for the coming kingdom, pointing beyond the present to what is yet to be.

And it is precisely for this reason that the Christian community should not only be living in hope, but acting in hope. In keeping that hope alive, the minister of the Word and Sacrament enables the People of God to witness to the kingdom and grow in the knowledge, grace and love of God.

Index of Names

Index of Names

171

Notes

PREFACE

1. G.C. Oosthuizen, J.K. Coetzee, J.W. de Gruchy, J.H. Hofmeyr, B.C. Lategan, *Religion, Intergroup Relations and Social Change in South Africa,* Pretoria, HSRC, 1985, p.109.
2. William R. Burrows, *New Ministries: The Global Context.* Maryknoll, New York, Orbis, 1981, p.3f.

CHAPTER ONE

1. Philip Schaff, ed., *Nicene and Post-Nicene Fathers of the Christian Church,* vol. ix, Grand Rapids, Eerdmans, 1889, reprinted 1983, p.9.
2. See Edward Farley, *Theologia: The Fragmentation and Unity of Theological Education,* Philadelphia, Fortress, 1983.
3. 'Novo incipiente nostro', 6 April, 1979, in Austin Flannery O.P. (ed.), *Vatican II: More Postconciliar Documents,* vol. II, Grand Rapids, Eerdmans, 1982, p.352.
4. See Eberhard Bethge, *Dietrich Bonhoeffer,* London, Collins, 1970, pp.103f; 470f.
5. See Dietrich Bonhoeffer, *Spiritual Care,* Philadelphia, Fortress, 1985, p.32f.
6. Stewart Ranson, Alan Bryman & Bob Hinings, *Clergy, Ministers & Priests,* London, Routledge & Kegan Paul, 1977, p.169.
7. H. Richard Niebuhr and Daniel D. Williams (eds.), *The Ministry in Historical Perspective,* New York, Harper & Row, 1983, p.309.
8. Joseph Hough and John Cobb, *Christian Identity and Theological Education,* Chico, California, Scholars Press, 1985, p.15.
9. Hans Kung, *Why Priests?,* London, Collins, 1972.
10. James N. Poling and Donald E. Miller, *Foundations for a Practical Theology of Ministry,* Nashville, Abingdon, 1985, p.19.
11. See Edward Schillebeeckx, *Ministry: A Case for Change,* London, SCM, 1981, p.66.
12. Thomas Franklin O'Meara, OP, *Theology of Ministry,* New York, Paulist Press, 1983, p.128, 95.
13. See Hough and Cobb, *Christian Identity,* p.5.
14. Bengt Sundkler, *The Christian Ministry in Africa,* London, SCM, 1960, p.304.
15. Sundkler, *The Christian Ministry in Africa,* p.309.

16. Edward Schillebeeckx, *The Church with the Human Face*, p.122.

17. Stephen C. Neill and Hans-Ruedi Weber, *The Layman in Christian History*, Philadelphia, Westminster, 1963, p.388.

18. Edward Schillebeeckx, *The Church with a Human Face*, p.121.

19. Hans Kung, *Why Priests?*, p.78.

20. *Baptism, Eucharist and Ministry*, Geneva, WCC, 1982, p.22.

21. Leonardo Boff, *Ecclesio-genesis*, London, Collins, 1986, p.66.

22. Hough and Cobb, *Christian Identity*, p.103.

23. Leonardo Boff, *Ecclesio-genesis*.

24. Nicholas Lash, *Theology on the Way to Emmaus*, London, SCM, 1986, p.199.

25. P.T. Forsyth, *The Church and the Sacraments*, London, Independent Press, 1953, p.70.

26. Lash, *Theology on the Way to Emmaus*, p.199.

27. See Hough and Cobb, *Christian Identity*, p.59ff.

28. See Edward Schillebeeckx, *The Church with a Human Face*, p.2, pp.40ff.

29. *The Kairos Document*, article 4.4, in *Journal of Theology for Southern Africa*, no. 53, December 1985, p.77. See below pp.61f.

30. Seward Hiltner, *Ferment in the Ministry*, Nashville, Abingdon, 1969, p.159.

31. See Helmut Thielicke, *A Little Exercise for Young Theologians*, Grand Rapids, Eerdmans, 1962, p.16f.

32. Dietrich Bonhoeffer, *True Patriotism*, London, Collins, 1973, p.28.

33. John T. McNeill, *A History of the Cure of Souls*, New York, Harper & Row, 1951, p.198.

34. Karl Barth, *Against the Stream: Shorter Post-War Writings, 1946-52*, London, SCM, 1954, p.8.

35. Theodore W. Jennings, jr., *The Vocation of the Theologian*, Philadelphia, Fortress, 1985.

36. Nicholas Lash, *Theology on the Way to Emmaus*, London, SCM, 1986, p.6.

37. David Tracy, *The Analogical Imagination: Christian Theology and the Culture of Pluralism*, London, SCM, 1981, p.14f.

38. Lash, *Theology on the Way to Emmaus*, p.7.

39. Karl Barth, *Church Dogmatics* I/1, Edinburgh, T & T Clark, 1969, p.xiii.

40. J. Miguez-Bonino, 'A View from Latin America', in Rex Ambler and David Haslam, *Agenda for Prophets: Towards a Political Theology for Britain*, London, Bowerdean Press, 1980, p.105.

41. Hough and Cobb, *Christian Identity*, p.80.
42. Karl Rahner, *Theological Investigations*, vol. ix, London, Darton, Longman & Todd, p.102.
43. Hough and Cobb, *Christian Identity*, p.92.
44. Dietrich Bonhoeffer, *Gesammelte Schriften*, Band 3, Eberhard Bethge (ed.), Munchen, Chr. Kaiser, 1966, p.421f.
45. See Ernst Feil, *The Theology of Dietrich Bonhoeffer*, Philadelphia, Fortress, 1985, p.28.
46. Farley, *Theologia*, p.31.
47. Farley, *Theologia*, p.39.
48. David Tracy, *The Foundations of Practical Theology*, in Don S. Browning, (ed.), *Practical Theology*, San Francisco, Harper & Row, 1983, p.66ff.
49. Cf. Jennings, *The Vocation of the Theologian*, p.2f.
50. Hough and Cobb, *Christian Identity*, p.4.
51. Gutierrez, *A Theology of Liberation*, p.6.
52. Frank Chikane, *The Incarnation in the Life of the People in Southern Africa*, in *Journal of Theology for Southern Africa*, no. 51, June 1985, pp.37ff.
53. Bonhoeffer, *Christology*, London, Collins, 1966, p.106.
54. See Albert Nolan, *Jesus before Christianity*, Cape Town, David Philip, 1976, p.136f.
55. Lewis W. Spitz, (ed.), *Luther's Works*, vol. 34, Philadelphia, Fortress, 1957, p.287f.
56. Karl Barth, *Evangelical Theology: An Introduction*, New York, Holt, Rinehart and Winston, 1963, p.71, p.77.
57. Martin Luther, in Harold J. Grimm, (ed.), *Luther's Works*, vol. 31, p.. 2.
58. Quoted in Bethge, *Dietrich Bonhoeffer*, p.471.
59. Paul Tillich, *The Shaking of the Foundations*, London, Penguin, 1964, p.123.
60. Karl Barth, *The Word of God and the Task of the Ministry*, New York, Harper, 1957, p.186.
61. Lash, *Theology on the Emmanus Road*, p.8.
62. Hugh Martin, *Puritanism and Richard Baxter*, London, SCM, 1954, p.191.
63. Thomas Long, 'Editorial', *Theology Today*, April 1985, vol. 42, no. 1, p.4.
64. A.M. Allchin, *Julian of Norwich and the Continuity of Tradition*, in Robert Llewelyn, (ed.), *Julian Woman of our Day*, London, Darton, Longman and Todd, 1985, p.30.
65. Karl Barth, *Evangelical Theology*, p.165.

CHAPTER TWO

1. *The Kairos Document, Challenge to the Church: A Theological Comment on the Political Crisis in South Africa*, published in *Journal of Theology for Southern Africa*, no. 53, December 1985, pp.61ff.

2. For a convenient summary and comprehensive bibliography, see C.H. Peisker, 'Prophet', in Colin Brown (ed.), *The New International Dictionary of New Testament Theology*, vol. 3, Exeter, Paternoster, 1978, pp.74ff.

3. Robin Gill, *Prophecy and Praxis*, London, Marshall, Morgan and Scott, 1981, p.14.

4. Stanley Hauerwas, 'The Pastor as Prophet: Ethical Reflections on an Improbable Mission', in Earl E. Shelp and Ronald H. Sunderland, *The Pastor as Prophet*, New York, Pilgrim Press, 1985, p.36.

5. Walter Brueggemann, 'Trajectories in Old Testament Literature and the Sociology of Ancient Israel', in Norman K. Gottwald (ed.), *The Bible and Liberation: Political and Social Hermeneutics*, New York, Orbis, 1984, p.308.

6. Brueggemann, in *The Bible and Liberation*, p.322.

7. Brueggemann, in *The Bible and Liberation*, p.325f.

8. Gregory Baum, *Religion and Alienation: A Theological Reading of Sociology*, New York, Paulist Press, 1975, p.194.

9. Guttierrez, *A Theology of Liberation*, p.11.

10. David E. Aune, *Prophecy in Early Christianity and the Ancient Mediterranean World*, Grand Rapids, Eerdmans, 1983, p.231. See also David Hill, *New Testament Prophecy*, London, Marshall, Morgan & Scott, 1979, p.2ff.

11. Aune, *Prophecy in Early Christianity*, p.198.

12. See Schillebeeckx, *The Church with a Human Face*, p.75.

13. Aune, *Prophecy in Early Christianity*, p.211; see also Hill, *New Testament Prophecy*, p.8.

14. See Eduard Schillebeeckx, *Jesus: An Experiment in Christology*, London, Collins, 1979, pp.234ff.

15. See James D.G. Dunn, *Christology in the Making: An Inquiry into the Origins of the Doctrine of the Incarnation*, London, SCM, 1980, esp. pp.137ff.

16. Hill, *New Testament Prophecy*, p.68.

17. See Karl Barth, *Church Dogmatics*, Vol. IV, Part 3, Edinburgh, T.&T. Clarke, 961, pp.11ff.

18. *Calvin's Geneva Catechism (1541)*, art. 38, T.F. Torrance (ed.), *The*

Notes

School of Faith: the Catechisms of the Reformed Church, London, James Clarke, 1959, p.11.

19. Barth, *Church Dogmatics*, Vol. IV, Part 3, p.52.

20. See Walter Brueggemann, *The Prophetic Imagination*, Philadelphia, Fortress, 1978, p.80ff.

21. See Schillebeeckx, *The Church with a Human Face*, p.71.

22. Aune, *Prophecy in Early Christianity*, p.338.

23. See Jurgen Moltmann, *The Trinity and the Kingdom of God*, London, SCM, 1981, esp. pp.191ff.

24. John Calvin, *The Institutes of the Christian Religion*, Book II, chap. xv, para. 1. John T. McNeill (ed.) The Library of Christian Classics, vol. xx, Philadelphia, Westminster, 1960, p.494.

25. See John Calvin, *Institutes of the Christian Religion*, Bk. 2, chap. 15, 1-2; cf. David W. Torrance and Thomas F. Torrance (eds.), *Calvin's New Testament Commentaries: Vol. 1*, Grand Rapids, Eerdmans, 1972, p.148.

26. Max Weber, *The Sociology of Religion*, Boston, Beacon Press, 1963, pp.60ff.

27. Kung, *The Church*, London, Burns & Oates, 1967, p.433.

28. Milan Machovec, *A Marxist Looks at Jesus*, London, Darton, Longman and Todd, 1976 p.193f.

29. Albert Nolan, 'Academic Freedom: A Service to the People', The Twenty-eighth T.B. David Memorial Lecture, University of Cape Town, July 31, 1986, published by the University, 1986, p.6f.

30. Daniel Jenkins, *The British: Their Identity and their Religion*, London, SCM, 1975, p.181.

31. Daniel W. Hardy and David F. Ford, *Jubilate: Theology in Praise*, London, Darton, Longman and Todd, 1984, p.40f.

32. Hardy and Ford, *Jubilate*, p.137.

33. *Preparing Today for Tomorrow's Ministry*, London, United Reformed Church, 1982, p.3.

34. *Preparing Today for Tomorow's Ministry*, p.4.

35. Gill, *Prophecy and Praxis*, p.42 et. al.

36. Gill, *Prophecy and Praxis*, p.20.

37. Ambler and Haslam, *Agenda for Prophets*, p.115.

38. Earl E. Shelp & Ronald H. Sunderland (eds.), *The Pastor as Prophet*, New York, Pilgrim Press, 1985.

39. Gill, *Prophecy and Praxis*, p.29, cf. pp.70, 73.

40. See Peter Hinchliff, *Holiness and Politics*, Grand Rapids, Eerdmans, 1983, p.141.

41. Stephen Yeo, 'Internal: Agenda for Prophets — Religion and What?', *Agenda for Prophets*, p.94.

42. Ambler 'On Looking Back into the Future', *Agenda for Prophets*, p.120.

43. Ronald Preston, 'Not out of the wood yet', *Theology*, March 1981.

44. Ronald Preston, *Church and Society in the Late Twentieth Century: The Economic and Political Task*, London, SCM, 1983, p.138.

45. Preston, *Church and Society*, p.107.

46. Dietrich Bonhoeffer, *No Rusty Swords*, London, Collins, 1965, p.161f.

47. Karl Barth, *Against the Stream*, p.47.

48. Joe Holland and Peter Henriot, S.J., *Social Analysis: Linking Faith and Justice*, New York, Orbis, 1984, p.7.

49. Holland and Henriot, *Social Analysis*, p.7f.

50. Holland and Henriot, *Social Analysis*, p.14.

51. Holland and Henriot, *Social Analysis*, p.13.

52. On the development of the concept *praxis*, see Richard J. Bernstein, *Praxis and Action*, Philadelphia, University of Pennsylvania Press, 1971.

53. Dietrich Bonhoeffer, *Das Wesen der Kirche*, Munich, Chr. Kaiser Verlag, 1971, p.58.

54. Hauerwas, in Shelp and Sunderland, *The Pastor as Prophet*, p.27.

55. J.P. Kiernan, 'Prophet and Preacher: An Essential Partnership in the Work of Zion', *Man*, vol. II, 1976, p.358.

56. Kiernan, in *Man*, p.363.

57. Brueggemann, *The Prophetic Imagination*, Philadelphia, Fortress, 1978, p.13.

58. West, *Bishop and Prophets*, pp.48ff.

59. Richard Fox, *Reinhold Niebuhr: A Biography*, New York, Pantheon, 1985, p.64.

60. Walter Brueggemann, *The Prophetic Imagination*, p.111f.

CHAPTER THREE

1. Edward Schillebeeckx, *Christ: the Experience of Jesus as Lord*, Crossroad, New York, 1981, p.724f.

2. See Johann Baptist Metz, *Faith in History and Society: Towards a Practical Fundamental Theology*, New York, Seabury, 1980, p.114.

3. But see Manas Buthelezi, 'Violence and the Cross in South Africa

Notes

Today', *Journal of Theology for Southern Africa*, no. 29, December 1979, pp.51f; T.A. Mofokeng, *The Crucified Among the Crossbearers*, Kampen, J.H. Kok, 1983, pp.227f.

4. Schillebeeckx, *Christ*, p.724.

5. Iulia de Beausobre, *Creative Suffering*, Westminster, Dacre Press, 1940, p.10f.

6. Schillebeeckx, *Christ*, p.671.

7. See especially John Hick, *Evil and the God of Love*, London, Collins, 1968.

8. Walter Eichrodt, 'Faith in Providence and Theodicy in the Old Testament', in James L. Crenshaw (ed.), *Theodicy in the Old Testament*, London, SPCK, 1983, pp.17ff.

9. P.T. Forsyth, *The Justification of God*, London, Independent Press, 1917, p.136.

10. Schillebeeckx, *Christ*, p.726.

11. See the recently published anthology, *The Return of the Amasi Bird: Black South African Poetry, 1881-1981*, edited by Tim Couzens and Essop Patel, Johannesburg, Raven Press, 1982.

12. An extract from Mongane Serote, *The Night Keeps Winking*, Gaberone, Botswana, p.7.

13. F. Nietzsche, *The Gay Science*, New York, Randon House, 1974, p.181.

14. Gerhard Tötemeyer, 'Detente or Aggression: South Africa's Policy in Southern Africa with special emphasis on Namibia.' Unpublished paper, University of Cape Town, 1985.

15. Quoted in John de Gruchy, *Cry Justice! Prayers, Meditations and Readings from South Africa*, London, Collins, 1986, p.199.

16. Eberhard Jungel, *God as the Mystery of the World*, Grand Rapids, Eerdmans, 1983, p.50.

17. Margaret Nash, *Black Uprooting from 'White' South Africa*, Johannesburg, SACC, 1980. Quoted in de Gruchy, *Cry Justice!* p.72f.

18. cf. Jurgen Moltmann, *The Crucified God*, London, SCM, 1974, p.221.

19. Jungel, *God as the Mystery of the World*, pp.49ff.

20. See the evocative study by Kornelis H. Miskotte, *When the Gods are Silent*, London, Collins, 1967.

21. Samuel E. Balentine, *The Hidden God: The Hiding of the Face of God in the Old Testament*, Oxford, Oxford University Press, 1983, p.171.

22. See Terence E. Fretheim, *The Suffering of God: An Old Testament Perspective*, Philadelphia, Fortress Press, 1984, p.65ff.

23. Abraham Heschel, *The Prophets*, vol. 1, New York, Harper & Row, 1955, p.218f.
24. Moltmann, *The Crucified God*, p.272.
25. Fretheim, *The Suffering God*, p.116, 120, 130, 136, 140.
26. Moltmann, *The Crucified God*, p.272.
27. Fretheim, *The Suffering of God*, p.108.
28. Dietrich Bonhoeffer, *Letters and Papers from Prison*, New York, Macmillan, 1972, p.348.
29. Kazoh Kitamori, *Theology of the Pain of God*, London, SCM, 1966.
30. Gordon D. Kaufman, 'Nuclear Eschatology and the Study of Religion', *Journal of the American Academy of Religion*, Vol. 51, no. 1, 1985.
31. See Jungel, *God as the Mystery of the World*, pp.55ff, p.65 note 26.
32. See Walther von Loewenich, *Luther's Theology of the Cross*, Belfast, Christian Journals Ltd., 1976.
33. See Moltmann, *The Crucified God*, p.229f.
34. Dorothee Soelle, *Suffering*, London, Darton, Longman and Todd, 1975, p.143.
35. cf. Jungel, *God as the Mystery of the World*, p.100.
36. Mofokeng, *The Crucified among the Crossbearers*, p.262.
37. Bonhoeffer, *Letters and Papers from Prison*, p.360f.
38. See Fretheim, *The Suffering of God*, p.144ff.
39. See Fretheim, *The Suffering of God*, p.166.
40. Bonhoeffer, *Letters and Papers from Prison*, p.362.
41. Moltmann, *The Crucified God*, 72f.
42. Metz, *Faith in History and Society*, p.115.
43. See for example, John Hick, *Evil and the Love of God*.
44. Nicholas Lash, *A Matter of Hope*, Notre Dame, University of Notre Dame Press, 1982, p.287.
45. Mofokeng, *The Crucified among the Crossbearers*, p.263.
46. Gustavo Gutierrez, *The Power of the Poor in History*, SCM, London, 1983. See also Kim Yong Bock, ed., *Minjung Theology: People as the Subjects of History*, New York, Orbis, 1981.

CHAPTER FOUR

1. Fritjof Capra, *The Turning Point*, London, Collins, Fontana, 1983, p.89.
2. See Colin Gunton, *Enlightenment & Alienation*, London, Marshall Morgan & Scott, 1985.

3. Gibson Winter, *Liberating Creation*, New York, Crossroad, 1981.

4. Capra, *The Turning Point*, p.289.

5. Capra, *The Turning Point*, p.290.

6. Capra, *The Turning Point*, p.291.

7. Hough and Cobb, *Christian Identity*, p.36.

8. Edward Farley, 'Theology and Practice Outside the Clerical Paradigm', in Browning, *Practical Theology*, p.34.

9. Jay C. Rochelle in Dietrich Bonhoeffer, *Spiritual Care*, Philadelphia, Fortress, 1985, p.7.

10. Nicholas Wolterstorff, *When Justice and Peace Embrace*, Grand Rapids, Eerdmans, 1983, p.81.

11. Stephen Sykes, *The Identity of Christianity*, London, SPCK, 1984, p.286.

12. See Bernard Lord Manning *Essays in Orthodox Dissent*, London, Independent Press, 1953; *The Making of Modern English Religion*, London, Independent Press, 1967.

13. Manning, *Essays in Orthodox Dissent*, p.117.

14. Gustavo Gutierrez, *A Theology of Liberation*, p.3.

15. Gutierrez, *A Theology of Liberation*, p.3.

16. F. Ross Kinsler, 'Equipping God's People for Mission', in *International Review of Mission*, vol. LXXI, no. 282, April 1982, p.134.

17. John Cobb, 'Theology as Thoughtful Response to the Divine Call' in Theodore Jennings, jr., (ed.), *The Vocation of the Theologian*, p.117.

18. See F. Ross Kinsler (ed.) *Ministry by the People: Theological Education by Extension*, Geneva, WCC; New York, Orbis, 1983; Robert L. Youngblood, (ed.) *Cyprus: TEE Come of Age*, London, Paternoster, 1986.

19. Hough and Cobb, *Christian Identity*, p.124.

20. Karl Barth, *The Word of God and Word of Man*, p.205.

21. Daniel Jenkins, *The British*, p.182.

22. See Sykes, *The Identity of Christianity*, pp.174ff.

23. See W.E. Sangster, *The Craft of the Sermon*, London, Epworth, 1954.

24. James S. Stewart, *Heralds of God*, London, Hodder & Stoughton, 1952; P.T. Forsyth, *Positive Preaching and the Modern Mind*, London, Independent Press, 1957.

25. P.T. Forsyth, *Positive Preaching*, p.1.

26. Allan Boesak, *The Finger of God: Sermons on Faith and Responsibility*, Johannesburg, Ravan, 1979, p.7.

27 Peter Stuhlmacher, *Historical Criticism and Theological Interpretation of Scripture*, Philadelphia, Fortress, 1977, p.90.

28. Leander Keck, *The Bible in the Pulpit*, Nashville, Abingdon, 1978, p.133; James M. Gustafson, *Theology and Ethics*, London, Blackwell, 1981, p.67.

29. Leander Keck, 'Toward a Theology of Rhetoric/Preaching', in Browning, *Practical Theology*, p.133f.

30. Juan Luis Segundo, *The Liberation of Theology*, New York, Orbis, 1976, p.8.

31. See Hans W. Frei, *The Eclipse of Biblical Narrative*, New Haven, Yale, 1974.

32. Stanley Hauerwas, *A Community of Character*, South Bend, Notre Dame, 1981, p.92.

33. See Hendrikus Berkhof, *Christian Faith*, Grand Rapids, Eerdmans, 1979, p.92.

34. Tracy, in Browning, *Practical Theology*, p.64.

35. Edward Farley and Peter C. Hodgson, 'Scripture and Tradition', in Peter C. Hodgson and Robert H. King, (eds.) *Christian Theology*, Philadelphia, Fortress, 1985, p.83f.

36. See Brian Gaybba, *The Tradition: An Ecumenical Breakthrough?* Rome, Herder, 1971, esp. pp.164ff. and pp.238ff.

37. See H.E.W. Turner, *The Pattern of Christian Truth*, London, Mowbray, 1954.

38. Henrikus Berkhof, *Christian Faith*, p.95.

39. Alisdair MacIntyre, *After Virtue*, South Bend, Notre Dame Press, 1981, p.206.

40. Rosemary Radford Reuther, 'Theology as Critique of and Emancipation from Sexism', in Jennings (ed.), *The Vocation of the Theologian*, p.31.

41. Richard E. Palmer, *Hermeneutics*, Evanston, Northwestern University Press, 1969, p.183.

42. Edward Farley, *Theologia*, p.167.

43. Gregory Baum, *Religion and Alienation*, New York, Paulist, 1975, p.222f.

44. See Allan A. Boesak, *Black and Reformed*, New York, Orbis, 1984; John W. de Gruchy, 'The Revitalization of Calvinism' in the *Journal of Religious Ethics*, June 1986.

45. Wolterstorff, *Until Justice and Peace Embrace*, p.176.

46. MacIntyre, *After Virtue*, p.207.

47. See Sally McFague, *Metaphorical Theology*, Philadelphia Fortress, 1983, p.120.

48. John Leith, *Introduction to the Reformed Tradition*, Atlanta, John

Notes

Knox, p.29.

49. Matthew Lamb, *Solidarity with Victims*, New York, Crossroads, 1982, p.96, n.77.

50. Lamb, *Solidarity with Victims*, p.53.

51. Robin Gill, *Prophecy and Praxis*, p.11.

52. Don Browning, *The Moral Context of Pastoral Care*, Philadelphia, Westminster, 1976, pp.109f.

53. Peter R. Williams, *Popular Religion in America*, Englewood-Cliffs, N.J., Prentice Hall, 1980, p.7.

54. Langdon Gilkey, in Jennings, *The Vocation of the Theologian*, p.98.

55. See Ronald Preston, *Church and Society*, p.14.

56. Browning, *The Moral Context*, p.98.

57. Bonhoeffer, *Spiritual Care*, p.32.

58. Browning, *The Moral Context*, p.100.

59. Walter Brueggemann, *The Prophetic Imagination*, p.110.

60. Brueggemann, *The Prophetic Imagination*, p.13.

61. Browning, *The Moral Context*, p.26.

62. Geoffrey Wainwright, *Doxology*, New York, Oxford, 1980, p.3.

63. Wainwright, *Doxology*, p.435.

64. Robert Bellah, *Beyond Belief: Essays on Religion in a Post-Traditional World*, New York, Harper & Row, 1970, p.211.

65. Hendrikus Berkhof, *Christian Faith*, p.377.

66. John A.T. Robinson, *On Being the Church in the World*, London, Mowbray, 1960, p.77.

67. Nicholas Wolerstorff, *Until Justice and Peace Embrace*, p.161.

68. See Allan Boesak and Charles Villa-Vicencio, *When Prayer Makes News*, Philadelphia, Westminster, 1986; John de Gruchy, *Cry Justice!*, pp.23ff.

69. Nicholas Lash, *A Matter of Hope*, p.205. See also p.239.